Modern
Icons

A SOURCE BOOK

This is a Flame Tree Book
First published in 2004

07 05 04 06

1 3 5 7 9 10 8 6 4 2

FLAME TREE PUBLISHING
Crabtree Hall, Crabtree Lane, Fulham,
London, SW6 6TY, United Kingdom
www.flametreepublishing.com

Flame Tree is part of
The Foundry Creative Media Company Limited

ISBN 1 84451 185 5 trade edition
ISBN 1 84451 212 6 plc edition

Printed in China

Special thanks to Anna Groves

Modern
Icons

A SOURCE BOOK

General Editor: Sonya Newland

FLAME TREE
PUBLISHING

CONTENTS

INTRODUCTION

There have been so many people who deserve the label 'icon' over the past one hundred years or so that it is difficult to know where to start making a selection for a volume like this one. Why should one person deserve the title more than another? And how should we even define the word itself? Perhaps they are the heroes and the martyrs – the people that risk their lives to save others or to stand up for a principle. Maybe they are those

who dedicate their lives to science or invention, changing our world for the better or increasing our understanding of it. Are they simply the people on whom we model ourselves – the people we would all secretly like to be? The answer, of course, is all of these – and then some.

There has not been a century like it in the history of the world. Before 1900, famous figures – the key people that others aspired to be – were rulers and politicians, those with tangible power. Some made their names in the arts, particularly literature and what we now call classical music, and some pioneering men began to question accepted rules of science, but they

◀ *LEFT: Winston Churchill, one of Britain's most influential statesmen.*

▼ *BELOW:* Le Pont Japonais, Bassin aux Nympheas, *one of the many works of art that Monet painted in his garden at Giverny.*

were not many and often failed to achieve recognition in their lifetimes. They also never reached the heights of fame and, more significantly, fortune in the way that those in the public eye do today.

As the twentieth century dawned, however, the world was standing on the brink of an era that would be like no other. The two World Wars are the obvious choices for events that made the twentieth century stand out – and there's nothing like war to create heroes. But there were other factors, too. Science – theoretical, physical and medical – had been working its way towards great discoveries and the first half of the century saw an explosion of new theories, developments and practices. Some pioneers also decided to test the new technology – and the human body – to its limits by going where no man had gone before: the South Pole; across the Atlantic in a plane; they even conquered the vast mysteries of space travel.

In the latter half of the century, as the world began to enjoy a new peace and found time to relax after the turmoil of the first 50 years, people became famous for other reasons. Rock 'n' roll shook the world in the 1950s and has now spawned several generations of musical icons. Filmmaking became a multi-million dollar industry and the actors and directors enjoyed their share of the fame and fortune. With the advent of television, sportsmen became global stars, garnering huge fan-bases and becoming household names.

In the confines of this definition of what makes an icon, there are some names that come immediately to mind: Martin Luther King, Winston Churchill, Thomas Edison, Muhammad Ali ... the list goes on; but there are others, perhaps less well-known outside their own countries, whose contributions and resulting status are no less deserving of mention. And of course, in the midst of all this discovery, change and new paths to fame, there were other people who came to the forefront of the

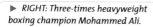

▶ *RIGHT: Three-times heavyweight boxing champion Mohammed Ali.*

global conscience. People who were not heroes, but still became inextricably entwined with different countries' histories and national identities. These personalities, whose power wreaked havoc and cruelty in our time and who are unmistakably the villains of the piece, must take their place as icons amongst those more worthy of admiration.

▶ RIGHT: Emmeline Pankhurst is arrested.

Now, nearly half way through the first decade of the twenty-first century, we take so many things for granted, and we forget that just about everything we do in our everyday lives – whether it's a trip to the doctor's for a dose of antibiotics, a holiday abroad, the act of voting in a local election, or simply revelling in the joy of our favourite tune – is down to somebody else's talent and tenacity. Without Alexander Fleming, Wilbur and Orville Wright, Emmeline Pankhurst and others like them, life might be very different.

As with all such things, the definition is subjective and inevitably there will be people who have been omitted in a volume of this size. We hope, however, that we have made a selection that is representative of all those people who made their mark on the world in some way over the past one hundred years, that your own hero or icon is here, and that you enjoy finding out about others who helped to shape the most revolutionary century in history.

ART & CULTURE

BACON, FRANCIS (1909–92)

Born in Dublin of English parents, Bacon left home at the age of 15, travelling to London, Berlin and Paris. In Paris he visited a Picasso exhibition, which inspired him to paint. In 1929, Bacon settled in London, where he designed Bauhaus-style furnishings and later, during wartime, joined the Civil Defence. His breakthrough as an artist came in 1945, when his *Three Studies for Figures at the Base of a Crucifixion* caused a sensation at the Lefevre Gallery. In this, as in many of his future works, elements of mutilation, pain and claustrophobia combined to create a highly disturbing effect.

From 1946 to 1950, Bacon resided in Monte Carlo. His international reputation growing, he returned to London. His source material was very diverse, ranging from the work of other artists (Velázquez, Van Gogh) to films and photographs (Muybridge, Eisenstein) and autobiographical details. Bacon's prevailing theme, however, is the vulnerability and solitude of the human condition.

◘ *see* Marc Chagall p. 18

BAILEY, DAVID (b. 1938)

Born in London, England, David Bailey grew up to become Britain's best-known photographer. Along with Terence Donovan, he captured, and in many ways helped create, the Swinging London of the 1960s: a culture of high fashion and celebrity chic. Both photographers socialized with actors, musicians and royalty, and found themselves elevated to star status. Together, they were the first real celebrity photographers. As well as fashion photography, Bailey has been responsible for record album sleeve

▶ *RIGHT: Eminent British photographer David Bailey with actress Catherine Deneuve in the 1960s.*

art, for performers including The Rolling Stones and Marianne Faithfull. In 1965, Bailey married the actress Catherine Deneuve; they were divorced in 1972. He subsequently married another actress, Catherine Dyer, in the 1980s. He was awarded the CBE in 2001.

◑ see The Rolling Stones p. 123

BARRIE, J. M. (1860–1937)

Scots playwright J. M. Barrie was born in 1860 in Kirriemuir, Angus, the son of a weaver. After a few years contributing articles and stories to London journals, Barrie turned dramatist in 1890. Fame came rapidly after he produced stage hits like *The Admirable Crichton* (1902), about an ingenious butler cast away with his master's family on a desert island, and Barrie's greatest and most enduring success, *Peter Pan* (1904). At its first performance, one admiring critic wrote: 'A capital entertainment full of droll imaginings, of such originality, tenderness and daring that [there was] no ... doubt regarding its complete success'.

◑ see George Bernard Shaw p. 71

BASQUIAT, JEAN-MICHEL (1960–88)

Jean-Michel Basquiat, of Puerto-Rican and Haitian parentage and born in Brooklyn, brought to his paintings his favourite boyhood obsessions: cars, weapons, war, old movies, Richard Nixon and J. Edgar Hoover, as well as referring to Cajun, Hispanic and black American culture. Basquiat used a combination of acrylic, oil paint and wax crayons, enclosing his simplified figures and symbols with white lines, like chalk on a blackboard. His figures' grimacing, skeletal faces, in paintings like *Profit I* (1982), recall the caricatural style of the French artist Jean Dubuffet, while his graffiti-like scratches and scribbles suggest an ironic take on 'primitive' art.

◑ see Francis Bacon p. 12

BETJEMAN, JOHN (1906–84)

English poet John Betjeman also worked as a teacher, journalist, broadcaster and expert critic of architecture. His first volume of poetry was published in 1931. Among his most famous works are: 'A Subaltern's Love Song', 'Myfanwy', 'Slough' and his autobiography, *Summoned by Bells*. He became Poet Laureate in 1972.

◆ *see* T. S. Eliot p. 25

BEUYS, JOSEPH (1921–86)

German conceptual artist Joseph Beuys drew heavily upon his German roots in the creation of a personal mythology. He served in the Luftwaffe during the World War II, and was shot down over the Crimea in 1943. His rescue by nomads was to shape his philosophy as an artist; the felt and fat in which they covered him endured as two of his favourite materials (expressing warmth and comfort), and their Shamanic beliefs influenced his view that the role of an artist was akin to that of a Shaman: channelling energy through objects to give them symbolic power.

◆ *see* Damien Hirst p. 32

BRAQUE, GEORGES (1882–1963)

Born in Argenteuil, the son of a house-painter, Braque was initially trained to carry on the family business. In 1902 he switched to art, but retained a profound respect for craftsmanship and always ground his own pigments. Initially, he joined the Fauvist group, but his style altered radically after two key events in 1907. Firstly he was overwhelmed by an exhibition of Cézanne's work, then, later in the year, he saw *Les Demoiselles d'Avignon* in Picasso's studio and embarked on a unique collaboration with the Spaniard. Working, in Braque's words, 'like two mountaineers roped together', they created Cubism. This artistic partnership was halted by the war, when Braque was called to the Front. He was decorated for bravery before being discharged with serious wounds in 1916. Unlike Picasso, who changed direction completely, Braque spent the remainder of his career refining his experiments with Cubism. These culminated in a magnificent cycle of paintings on *The Studio*, which he began in 1947. Braque also diversified into design work, producing ballet décors, stained-glass windows, book illustrations and, most notable of all, a ceiling for the Etruscan Gallery in the Louvre.

◑ *see* Paul Cézanne p. 17

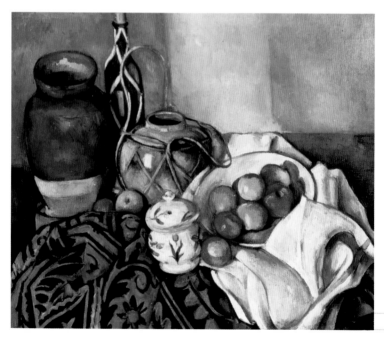

BRITTEN, BENJAMIN (1913–76)

The finest English composer of his generation, Britten reacted against the folksong-derived pastoralism of his elder compatriots, finding inspiration in Purcell and influences as various as Mahler and Stravinsky. The international success of his opera *Peter Grimes* (1945) brought financial security, but he continued to appear as a pianist, accompanying his partner, the tenor Peter Pears. He both founded and actively directed the English Opera Group at the Aldburgh Festival.

◆ *see* Igor Stravinsky p. 73

CAMUS, ALBERT (1913–60)

French writer Albert Camus was originally a philosophy student and this early interest is evident in many of his works. Camus' writings look at subjects such as the paradox of life and death. *L'Étranger* (1942) and *La Chute* (1956) are among his best-known books.

◆ *see* Marcel Proust p. 59

CÉZANNE, PAUL (1839–1906)

Cézanne is considered by many art critics to be the 'father of modern art'. He trained in Paris and together with Pissarro exhibited in the first Impressionist exhibition in 1874. However Cézanne's own critical success came later, once he had rejected Impressionism. Though still representational, Cézanne moved toward a more abstract art, with his use of colour and shape reflecting the internal reactions he felt about the images he was depicting, rather than attempting a realistic portrayal. This stylistic development led to the Cubists of the early twentieth century.

◆ *see* Marcel Duchamp p. 23

◀ *LEFT: Paul Cézanne's* Still Life With Apples *(1893–94).*

▶ *RIGHT: Renowned French fashion designer Coco Chanel.*

CHAGALL, MARC (1887–1975)

Born into an Orthodox Jewish family in what was then known as Russian Poland, Chagall studied in St Petersburg and Paris and returned to his native city on the eve of World War I. On his return to Russia he joined the Knave of Diamond group and participated in their 1917 exhibition, which was intended as an attack on the stuffy classicism of the Moscow School of Art. The Revolution broke out shortly afterwards and Chagall was appointed Director of the Vitebsk Art School before being summoned to Moscow to design sets for the Jewish Theatre. He left Russia in 1922 and settled near Paris. On the outbreak of World War II he moved to the USA. His paintings combine fantasy, folklore and biblical themes with an intensely surreal quality.

◆ *see* Paul Cézanne p. 17

CHANEL, COCO (1883–1971)

Coco Chanel was born Gabrielle Bonheur Chanel in the small city of Saumur, France. She was born out of wedlock to destitute parents. When she was 12, her mother died of malnutrition and overwork. Shortly afterwards, Coco's father abandoned her and her siblings. From such inauspicious beginnings, she would become one of the most influential figures in *haute couture* in the twentieth century. Two of her most famous creations are the Chanel No. 5 perfume, still a classic fragrance today, and the Chanel suit: an elegant outfit with boxy lines, made of pastel pink wool with black trim and gold buttons, worn with large costume-pearl necklaces. She spent the latter years of her life alone in Lausanne, Switzerland and is buried there, her tomb surrounded by five stone lions.

◆ *see* Mary Quant p. 60

CLOSE, CHUCK (b. 1940)

Chuck Close studied art at Yale from 1962 to 1964 and settled in New York City in 1967. In that year, influenced by the photographic self-portraits produced by Claude Cahun in the 1920s, he began painting photographs of portraits, meticulously reproducing the tiniest detail. Every line and wrinkle, every pore and individual strands of hair are carefully delineated. In fact, appearances can be deceptive; closer examination often reveals slight distortion or blurring around the ears or shoulders in order to convey the impression that the face is looming towards the viewer. In this way the artist remedies the shortcomings of the camera lens. In more recent years he has taken this a stage further, combining this photo-realism with such techniques as finger-painting, a microscopic stippled effect and collages.

◆ *see* Andy warhol p. 75

COPLAND, AARON (1900–90)

Born in Brooklyn of Russian Jewish parentage, Copland became the archetypal composer of the American West, his style much imitated by the writers of Hollywood film scores. Trained in Paris by Nadia Boulanger, he was strongly influenced by Stravinsky and began using jazz elements in early works. His next and most familiar phase was a more popular style, using folk music, including cowboy songs, in the ballets *Billy the Kid* (1938) and *Rodeo* (1942).

◆ *see* Igor Stravinsky p. 73

DAHL, ROALD (1916–90)

Roald Dahl was born in Llandaff, Glamorgan, Wales, to Norwegian parents. He served as a fighter pilot in the British Royal Air Force during World War II, and during his service he was shot down in the Libyan Desert and

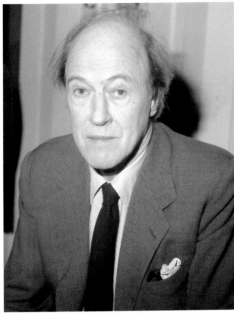

◀ *LEFT: Leading children's writer Roald Dahl.*

severely injured. He began writing in 1942 when he was transferred to Washington, DC, as Assistant Air Attache. His first published short story was *A Piece of Cake*, describing his accident in Libya. Dahl went on to write children's stories, many illustrated by Quentin Blake, including the classics *Charlie and the Chocolate Factory* (1964) and *James and the Giant Peach* (1961). He also wrote macabre adult fiction. One of his more famous adult stories, *The Smoker*, was filmed as an episode of *Alfred Hitchcock Presents*.

◖ *see* Alfred Hitchcock p. 104

DALÍ, SALVADOR (1904–89)

Dalí was born in Catalonia and studied at the Academy of Fine Arts in Madrid, until his outrageous behaviour caused his expulsion. In the early 1920s, he dabbled in a variety of styles, including Futurism and Cubism, although it was the metaphysical paintings of De Chirico that made the deepest impact on him.

The key stage in Dalí's career came in 1929, when he made *Un Chien Andalou* with Buñuel, met his future wife Gala, and allied himself with the Surrealists. His relationship with the latter was rarely smooth and, after several clashes with Breton, he was forced out of the group in 1939. In the interim, he produced some of the most memorable and hallucinatory images associated with the movement, describing them as 'hand-painted dream photographs'. Dalí remained very much in the public eye in later years, gaining great celebrity and wealth in the US, but for many critics his showmanship overshadowed his art.

⬍ *see* Antonio Gaudi p. 28

▲ *ABOVE: Salvador Dali with one of his works,* A Soft Self Portrait.

DEGAS, EDGAR (1834–1917)

French Artist Edgar Degas began his career as a historical painter but soon moved to contemporary subjects. His work was included in most of the Impressionist Exhibitions of the late-nineteenth century, but he does not easily fit into this category. Degas' most celebrated works contain scenes of dancers or women at work or at their toilette. He was interested in the exploration of movement that these scenes offered and in attempting to capture moments from everyday life. Some of Degas' paintings proved controversial – many people were offended by the realism and modernity of his work.

◆ *see* Claude Monet p. 50

DOMINGO, PLACIDO (b. 1941)

Spanish opera star Placido Domingo started his career as a baritone in 1959, but the following year performed one of the great tenor roles, the hero Alfredo in Verdi's *La Traviata*. Since then, Domingo has become one of the most acclaimed opera singers in the world, performing varied roles in operas by Verdi, Puccini and Wagner. As an opera star, Domingo has it all: good looks and impressive acting ability as well as a powerful, lyrical voice. Domingo, who is also a pianist and conductor, has worked to make opera more accessible to non-opera goers. He has made numerous records of popular songs and has appeared in the 'Three Tenors' concerts with Luciano Pavarotti and José Carreras. (*See over for illustration.*)

◆ *see* Luciano Pavarotti p. 55

DUCHAMP, MARCEL (1887–1968)

Although he produced relatively few artworks, Duchamp was a key figure in twentieth-century art, playing a seminal role in the development of several different movements. Duchamp trained in Paris, and was briefly

◀ LEFT: Spanish opera singer and one of the Three Tenors, Placido Domingo.

influenced by Cézanne and the Fauves. His first real masterpiece – *Nude Descending a Staircase* – was a potent blend of Cubism and Futurism. In 1913 he invented the *ready-made* – an everyday object, divorced from its normal context and presented as a work of art in its own right. Two years later, Duchamp moved to the US, where he became a leading light of the New York Dada movement. His work from this period displayed a mischievous sense of humour, whilst also challenging existing preconceptions about the nature of art. His most notorious *ready-made* was a urinal, which he exhibited under the title of *Fountain*. After receiving a legacy, Duchamp's output slowed dramatically but his later work has been seen as a foretaste of Kinetic art and Conceptual art.

◄► *see* Paul Cézanne p. 17

ELIOT, T. S. (1888–1965)

Eliot was an American poet, playwright and critical essayist who moved to England in 1915. He worked as a schoolteacher, a bank clerk, a book reviewer, a book editor and a director of Faber and Faber publishers. His first published poem was 'The Love Song of J. Alfred Prufrock' (1915). His first volume of poetry was published in 1917. He was friends with Ezra Pound and Virginia Woolf. His poetry includes *The Waste Land* (1922) and *Old Possum's Book of Practical Cats* (1939, on which the musical *Cats* is based). Amongst his plays are *Murder in the Cathedral* (1935, about the martyr Thomas Becket) and *Sweeney Agonistes* (1923). Eliot was awarded the Nobel Prize for Literature in 1948.

◄► *see* John Betjemen p. 15

▶ RIGHT: *Nobel Prize winner T. S. Eliot.*

EMIN, TRACEY (b. 1963)

British artist Tracey Emin uses objects and installations in her intensely personal and autobiographical work, such as *Everyone I Have Ever Slept With* (1995), which gave a history of her sex life.

⬖ *see* Damien Hirst p. 32

FOSTER, NORMAN (b. 1935)

Sometime partner of Richard Rogers, the English architect Norman Foster was renowned for his precise and gracious buildings, such as his 1970s design for the Willis-Faber-Dumas Offices in Ipswich.

⬖ *see* Frank Lloyd Wright p. 77

FRANK, ANNE (1929–45)

Anne Frank was a Dutch Jewish girl whose diaries record the two years she and her family spent hiding from the Nazis in occupied Amsterdam during World War II. Anne and her family were eventually captured and she died in Belsen concentration camp just before it was liberated at the end of the war. Her diary brought home to the world the horrors experienced by Jews persecuted in occupied countries at this time.

⬖ *see* Adolf Hitler p. 248

FREUD, LUCIAN (b. 1922)

Freud was born in Berlin, the grandson of the famous psychoanalyst Sigmund Freud. As a Jewish family living in the shadow of Nazism, the Freuds left in the 1930s, settling in London. Lucian joined the Merchant Navy, becoming an artist after he was invalided out of the service in 1942. He trained under Cedric Morris, and the hallucinatory realism of his early

▶ RIGHT: *World-famous diarist Anne Frank.*

style hints at an admiration for Surrealism and Neue Sachlichkeit. His greatest influence, however, was Ingres. Freud emulated the meticulous draughtsmanship of the Frenchman, apparently attempting to depict every strand of hair on his sitters.

His virtuoso skill was recognized when, in 1951, his remarkable *Interior at Paddington* won a prize at the Festival of Britain.

Freud's style changed in the late 1950s, when he replaced his fine sable brushes with stiffer, hog-hair ones which led to a more painterly approach, in which the artist conveyed his flesh-tones through thicker slabs of colour. Freud's favourite subject matter has been the 'naked portrait': starkly realistic nudes, devoid of any picturesque or idealizing elements.

◘ *see* Sigmund Freud p. 274

GAUDI, ANTONIO (1852–1926)

Architect Antonio Gaudi's work can be seen in his home town of Barcelona. Although the impact of the current Art Nouveau movement was evident in Gaudi's work, he was clearly more affected by the Gothic, Moorish and Moroccan architectural styles. Gaudi's development of his inimitable and highly original style was aided by the extensive commissions he received from the industrialist Count Güell; Palau Güell and Park Güell are two of Gaudi's most astonishing buildings. Gaudi's style was heavily ornate, fantastical and included elements of the macabre. His work has been extensively inspirational, most notably for artists such as Salvador Dali.

◘ *see* Salavdor Dali p. 21

◀ LEFT: *The Guggenheim Museum in Bilbao, designed by Frank Gehry.*

GEHRY, FRANK (b. 1929)

American architect Frank Gehry's work includes the California Aerospace Museum, Los Angeles, and the Guggenheim Museum, Bilbao. Gehry's style is both innovative and provocative.

◆ see Frank Lloyd Wright p. 77

GERSHWIN, GEORGE (1898–1937)

As a teenager, Gershwin played the latest hit songs to potential customers in a sheet-music store, and by the age of 21 he had become a successful songwriter himself. After a visit to Europe, he began writing musicals, but also sought a formal musical education, studying briefly with numerous teachers. Alongside his musicals and popular songs, he began to write concert works, beginning with *Rhapsody in Blue* (1942). *An American in Paris* (1927) is a still more successful example of this, but Gershwin's ambition now was to combine his command of large-scale forms and his mastery of musical theatre in a genuinely American opera. This he achieved, two years before his death, with *Porgy and Bess* (1935), but his popular songs have proved no less enduring.

◆ see Aaron Copeland p. 21

GIACOMETTI, ALBERTO (1901–66)

Alberto Giacometti studied in Geneva but worked mostly in Paris, where he settled in 1922, spending some time as a sculptor with Antoine Bourdelle. He moved in the intellectual circle dominated by Jean-Paul Sartre and was an enthusiastic disciple of Existentialism.

In his painting he was originally drawn to the Cubists but in 1930 he embraced Surrealism as preached by André Breton, although he was expelled from the movement five years later. This was a defining moment, which resulted in a radical departure from previous styles and the evolution of strange, wraith-like figures. Although he is best remembered as a sculptor for his semi-abstract bronzes such as the *Thin Man* series and even more skeletal, spidery figures of the immediate postwar period, the same qualities are evident in his paintings – mostly portraits of real people executed in an abstract fashion.

◘ *see* John-Paul Sartre p. 69

GILBERT (b. 1943) and GEORGE (b. 1942)

Italian-born Gilbert Proesch first met George Pasmore when they were both students at St Martin's School of Art in London and have worked together since graduating in 1969. George had previously studied at Dartington Hall and the Oxford School of Art, while Gilbert had attended the Academy of Art in Munich. Since the late 1960s they have worked as performance artists, principally as living sculptures, their faces and hands covered with gold paint and holding the same pose for hours on end.

Subsequently they developed two-dimensional art, often comprising a series of framed photographs which are integrated to form a single entity. Their very conservative images in these collaborative works often clash with the subject matter, in which bodily functions and overt references to homosexuality feature prominently. Controversy surrounds their work, which is often seen as promoting rather than condemning fascist or racist attitudes, although they claim to be attempting to define the 'new morality'.

◘ *see* Roy Lichtenstein p. 39

▲ ABOVE: *Contemporary performance artists Gilbert and George.*

GLASS, PHILIP (b.1937)

Glass studied with Nadia Boulanger and Alla Rakha, but the influence of Indian music is not overt in his own pieces, rather it is evident in the additive, repetitive rhythmic processes. Parallel lines, simple diatonic harmony and unspecified instrumentation are characteristic of Glass's early music. Glass had a productive association with Hollywood, creating scores for films including *The Truman Show* (1999) and the Oscar-nominated *The Hours* (2003).

see Arnold Schoenberg p. 71

GROPIUS, WALTER (1883–1969)

German architect Walter Gropius created the Bauhaus school at Weimar in 1919. Taking his inspiration from William Morris, the Expressionists and the Arts and Crafts movement, Gropius believed that through architecture a powerful unity between artists and crafts people could be created. By 1923 Gropius turned his focus upon industrial design. Gropius left the Bauhaus in 1928.

see Frank Lloyd Wright p. 77

HIRST, DAMIEN (b. 1965)

British artist Damien Hirst's work is filled with images of death such as 1993's infamous *Mother and Child Divided* (a bisected cow and calf). Despite his unusual approach to art, Hirst won the 1995 Turner Prize and continues to attract controversy.

see Tracey Emin p. 26

HOCKNEY, DAVID (b. 1937)

Hockney was born in Bradford, Yorkshire, and trained at the Royal College of Art. There, his fellow students included Allen Jones, Derek

▲ ABOVE: British Pop artist David Hockney in 1969.

Boshier and R. B. Kitaj, and together they exhibited at the Young Contemporaries exhibition of 1961, a landmark show that marked the arrival of British Pop Art. Hockney himself denies belonging to this movement, even though his early work contained many references to popular culture. Instead, his style may be better defined as New Figuration – a blanket term, relating to the revival of figurative art in the 1960s.

Hockney has travelled widely in Europe throughout his career, but his main passion has been for the United States, especially Los Angeles, where he settled in 1976. Throughout his career, autobiographical subjects have featured heavily in his paintings, ranging from friends, such as the Clarks, lovers sunbathing by swimming pools, to an entire book of pictures devoted to his dogs. Hockney has also been a prolific stage designer, creating sets and costumes for *The Rake's Progress*, *The Magic Flute* and *Parade*. In recent years, he has also experimented with photo-work, producing elaborate 'photocollages' from hundreds of photographic prints.

◆ *see* Gilbert and George p. 30

JOYCE, JAMES (1882–1941)

The Irish writer James Joyce was hugely influential and innovative. He was one of the pioneers of the stream-of-consciousness style of writing in the 1920s, evidenced in his novel *Ulysses* (1922). Joyce's work was a great catalyst for change within twentieth-century literature, although some have accused it of being inaccessible.

◆ *see* T. S. Eliot p. 25

▶ *RIGHT: Russian expressionist painter Wassily Kandinsky.*

KANDINSKY, WASSILY
(1866–1944)

The Russian-born painter and art theoretician Wassily Kandinsky founded the *Blaue Reiter* ('Blue Rider') group with fellow painter Franz Marc in Berlin in 1911. Linked to the Expressionist style by his work with *Blaue Reiter*, Kandinsky is also reputed to have created the first truly abstract painting in 1910, although his work still retained elements of representation for another decade or so.

◆ *-see* Paul Klee p. 37

▲ ABOVE: Mexican artist Frida Kahlo with her artist husband Diego Rivera.

KAHLO, FRIDA (1907–54)

Born at Coyoicoan near Mexico City, Frida Kahlo had the misfortune to be in a streetcar crash at the age of 15. During her long convalescence she took up painting and submitted samples of her work to Diego Rivera, whom she married in 1928. Artistic temperament resulted in a stormy relationship that ended in divorce in 1939, and many of Kahlo's self-portraits in this period are wracked with the pain she suffered all her adult life, as well as reflecting anger at her husband's numerous infidelities. Indeed, pain and the suffering of women in general were dominant features of her paintings, endlessly explored and revisited in canvasses that verge on the surreal and often shock with their savage intensity.

◆ *see* Diego Rivera p. 62

KEYNES, JOHN MAYNARD (1883–1946)

English economist, financier and journalist John Maynard Keynes studied at Eton and Cambridge then worked in the India Office, examining pre-World War I Indian finance. He was an economic adviser at the Versailles Peace Conference and wrote *The Economic Consequences of the Peace* (1919) and *The General Theory of Employment, Interest and Money* (1936). In 1944 he was the Chief British Representative at the Bretton Woods Conference and negotiated the 1945 loan from the USA to Britain.

◆ *see* Jean-Paul Sartre p. 69

KLEE, PAUL (1879–1940)

Paul Klee studied in Munich and worked there as an etcher. In 1911 he joined with Feininger, Kandinsky and Jawlensky in the *Blaue Reiter* group founded by August Macke; up to that time he had worked mainly in watercolours, painting in an Expressionist manner with overtones of

Blake and Beardsley, but subsequently he veered towards Cubism under the influence of Robert Delaunay and from 1919 onwards painted mostly in oils. In 1920 he became a teacher at the Bauhaus and in the ensuing period his paintings mingled the figural with the abstract as he explored subtle combinations of colours and shapes, often deriving elements from folk art and even children's drawings. He severed his connections with the Bauhaus and returned to Switzerland when the Nazis came to power in 1933 and condemned his works as degenerate art.

◆ *see* Wassily Kandinsky p. 35

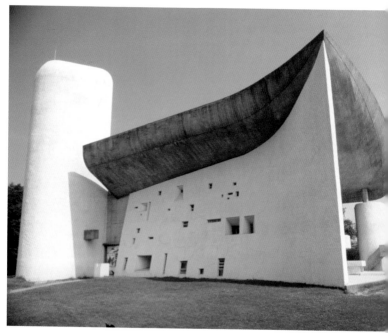

LAWRENCE, THOMAS EDWARD (1888–1935)

T. E. Lawrence was a British soldier and scholar. He earned the nickname 'Lawrence of Arabia' after he was based in Cairo with British military intelligence, where he became guerrilla leader of the Arab revolt against Turkish rule during World War I. After writing a history of the revolt in *Seven Pillars of Wisdom*, he changed his name twice and withdrew to obscurity. He was killed in a bike accident in 1935.

◆ *see* Wilfred Owen p. 55

LE CORBUSIER (1887–1965)

Le Corbusier was the pseudonym of Charles Edouard Jeanneret. He was an architect famous for what is now known as the International Style, along with Ludwig Mies van der Rohe, Walter Gropius and Theo van Doesburg. The International Style was a major architectural trend in the 1920s and 1930s and is the most minimal form of modernism. He was born in Switzerland but moved to Paris, France at the age of 29 and adopted 'Le Corbusier', his maternal grandfather's name, as a pseudonym.

◆ *see* Ludwig Mies van der Rohe p. 64

LICHTENSTEIN, ROY (1923–97)

Roy Lichtenstein enrolled at the Art Students' League (1939) and later studied at Ohio State College. After military service (1943–46) he returned to Ohio State as a teacher, and later taught at New York State and Rutgers Universities. He began exhibiting in 1949, his early works inspired by aspects of American history, strongly influenced by Cubism, though later he tended towards Abstract Expressionism. While teaching at Rutgers he met Allan Kaprow, who opened his eyes to the artistic possibilities

◀ *LEFT: The Chapel of Notre Dame du Haut, designed by Le Corbusier in 1956.*

inherent in consumerism and from about 1960 he developed what later came to be known as Pop Art, in which images are painted in the style of the comic strip. Even the dots of the screening process used in the production of comic books is meticulously reproduced in Lichtenstein's highly stylized paintings.

 see Andy Warhol p. 75

MACKINTOSH, CHARLES RENNIE (1868–1928)

Scottish architect Mackintosh, together with his future wife Margaret MacDonald, was a leader of the Glasgow Group. The group produced both architectural plans and interior designs, such as furniture and metalwork. Mackintosh combined beliefs taken from the Arts and Crafts Movement with elements of the Pre-Raphaelites and Japanese art into his own unique blend of Art Nouveau. Both in Britain and Europe, Mackintosh's designs brought him much acclaim and in 1897 he won the competition to design the new Glasgow School of Art. The building was one of the highlights of his career, beautifully combining a complex rationale with widespread influences, such as Scottish castles.

◆ see Frank Lloyd Wright p. 77

MAGRITTE, RENÉ (1898–1967)

The great Surrealist master René François Ghislain Magritte studied at the Académie Royale des Beaux-Arts in Brussels (1916–18) and became a commercial artist for fashion magazines and a designer of wallpaper. His paintings were initially influenced by Futurism and Cubism, but later he was attracted to the work of Giorgio de Chirico. In 1924 he became a founder member of the Belgian Surrealist group, which provided an escape from the dull routine of his everyday work. From 1927 to 1930 he lived in Paris to better continue his study of the Surrealists, then returned to Brussels where he built his reputation for paintings of dreamlike incongruity, in which themes and objects are jumbled in bizarre, nonsensical situations, often showing paintings within paintings. He is regarded in the United States as a forerunner of Pop Art.

◆ see Salvador Dalí p. 21

◀ LEFT: An interior design by Scottish artist Charles Rennie Mackintosh.

◄ *LEFT: Henry Matisse's* Blue Nude I *and* Flowing Hair *at a 2002 exhibition at the Tate Modern Gallery in London.*

MALEVICH, KASIMIR (1878–1935)

Kasimir Severinovich Malevich studied in Moscow from 1902 to 1905 and came under the influence of the French Impressionists. In 1912 Mikhail Larionov invited him to take part in the inaugural Knave of Diamonds exhibition. Later the same year he visited Paris and immediately converted to Cubism, attacking this new style with zeal and improving and refining it in a style which he called Suprematism. His exhibition of Suprematist art in 1915 gained a mixed reception and he subsequently modified his style, rejecting the stark minimalism of such works as *Black Square* and injecting a great deal of colour. But he reverted to his ideals in 1918 with a series of paintings entitled *White on White*, the ultimate example of minimalism. Thereafter he abandoned painting and concentrated on sculpture, becoming one of the leading Constructivists of the early Soviet era.

◘ *see* Pablo Picasso p. 56

MATISSE, HENRI (1869–1954)

Originally a law student, the French artist Henri Matisse had relatively little formal training and this is reflected in the naiveté of his work. Taking on board influences of the Post-Impressionists, Paul Cézanne and Vincent van Gogh, Matisse was the instigator of Fauvism (*fauve* meaning 'wild beast'). His exploration of colour parallels the Cubists' exploration of form. Matisse's palette is vivid and extreme, colour dominates his paintings. Sometimes criticized for his exclusion of negative subjects, Matisse once wrote that he wanted his art to be like a 'good armchair'. His subjects were mostly figures and landscapes. One of his most popular paintings was *Joi de Vivre* (1905–06).

◘ *see* Paul Cézanne p. 17

◀ LEFT: British Punk band The Sex Pistols, managed by Malcom McLaren.

McLAREN, MALCOLM (b. 1946)

An impresario and self-publicist, Malcolm McLaren was the manager
of the punk rock band the Sex Pistols, having discovered them in 1976
while managing the 'Sex' clothes shop with fashion designer Vivienne
Westwood in London's Kings Road. Prior to this, he had managed the New
York Dolls. He also formed and managed early 1980s pop group Bow Wow
Wow and is sometimes credited with developing the talents of Adam Ant
and Boy George. McLaren also released some work under his own name,
most notably an album *Duck Rock* (1983), which drew on musical styles
from North America and South Africa, among others. The tracks 'Buffalo
Girls' and 'Double Dutch' became chart hits in the UK.

↕ see Vivienne Westwood p. 76

MESSIAEN, OLIVIER (1908–92)

French composer Messiaen's music is unmistakeably personal, drawn
from a wide range of interests rather than influences. A church organist
from his twenties, he investigated church and other modes, studied
Asian and ancient Greek music and was an insatiable collector of
birdsong. Central to his work was his Roman Catholic faith, but secular
and personal concerns also surfaced in his ecstatic love songs, addressed
to his first wife, and others.

↕ see Igor Stravinsky p. 73

MILLER, GLENN (1904–44)

Born in Iowa, Miller was one of America's most celebrated bandleaders.
He produced distinctive arrangements that included a strong saxophone
element. Miller muted the brass section of his orchestra in a way that

helped produce the unique sound that was his signature, although it took him a long time to form a viable orchestra of his own. He finally launched his own band in 1938, and its highly individual sound made it instantly popular – so much so that the Glenn Miller Orchestra remained at the top of the charts throughout their entire career. By 1940 Miller's band had its own radio programme and was soon making films.

The same year, shortly after the US entered World War II, Miller disbanded his orchestra and joined the US Army Air Force, intent on active service. Instead, he was persuaded to make his contribution by boosting morale with his music. The orchestra reformed and over the next two years played on radio and in war zones in the Pacific, Europe and Britain. On 16 December 1944, Miller flew across the English Channel to France. He never arrived. No distress signal was received and no wreckage was ever found. Miller's disappearance remains a mystery to this day.

◆ see Amelia Earhart p. 306

MIRÓ, JOAN (1893–1983)

Spanish painter, ceramist and graphic artist and a key member of the Surrealists, Miró trained under Francisco Galí. His early work showed traces of Fauvism and Cubism, but his first one-man show was a disaster. Undeterred, Miró decided to travel to Paris, the acknowledged home of the avant-garde. There, he contacted Picasso, who introduced him to the most radical artists and poets of the day. These included the blossoming Surrealist group, which Miró joined in 1924.

Miró was fascinated by the challenge of using art as a channel to the subconscious and, from the mid-1920s, he began to fill his canvasses with biomorphic, semi-abstract forms. Nevertheless, he felt suspicious

▶ RIGHT: Big Band leader Glenn Miller.

46

of some of the more outlandish Surrealist doctrines and remained at the fringes of the group. He moved to France during the Spanish Civil War, producing patriotic material for the struggle against Francisco Franco, but was obliged to return south in 1940 after the Nazi invasion. By this stage, Miró's work was much in demand, particularly in the US, where he received commissions for large-scale murals. Increasingly, these featured ceramic elements, which played a growing part in the artist's later style.

◆ *see* Pablo Picasso p. 56

MODIGLIANI, AMEDEO (1884–1920)

Amedeo Modigliani was born into a Jewish family in Livorno, Italy. Although he was educated in the Italian centres of Florence and Venice he spent most of his career in France. His highly individual style combined the linear elegance of Botticelli, whose work he had studied in Italy, with the avant-garde ideas that were circulating in pre-war Paris. The key influence was the Romanian sculptor Brancusi, whom he met in 1909. After the outbreak of war, the raw materials for sculpture became scarce, so Modigliani turned to painting. Most of his subjects were sensual nudes or portraits, featuring slender, elongated figures. These received little attention from the critics; he was better known for his self-destructive, bohemian lifestyle, a lifestyle which caused the breakdown of his health. Modigliani died of tuberculosis at the age of 35. Modigliani's reputation was only secured posthumously, through a retrospective exhibition in Paris in 1922.

◆ *see* Claude Monet p. 50

◀ LEFT: *The studio of Spanish artist Joan Miró in Palma, Mallorca.*

MONDRIAN, PIET (1872–1944)

Born Pieter Cornelis Mondriaan, he simplified his name in 1909 when he moved to Paris, where he came under the influence of the Cubists, notably Henri Matisse. From still life, his work became progressively more abstract, his paintings distinguished by tightly regimented geometric shape and contrasting bright colours. In 1917 he became a founder member of De Stijl, the movement that derived its name from the journal which provided a forum for the Dutch avant-garde artists. Through this medium he propounded the theories which had a profound effect on a later generation as well as his contemporaries, and led to the development of the movement known as Neoplasticism. Mondrian was the arch-apostle of the abstract in its purest, simplest form. He moved to London in 1938, but after his studio was destroyed in the Blitz he settled in New York.

◆ see Henri Matisse p. 43

MONET, CLAUDE (1840–1926)

Amongst the Impressionist painters, Monet appears to exemplify the ideals of the movement best. Eugène Boudin convinced Monet to paint in the open air and by 1864 he had begun to work on landscapes with an eye to the atmosphere that they evoked. Monet's life's work was the study of nature and the effect of light upon it. Famed for his many series of paintings, such as *Haystacks*, Monet revisited the same scene or subject at different times of day and in different seasons to capture light fluctuations. Monet's final works were impacted by his encroaching blindness and with their vagueness they were both a great influence upon, and a pre-emption of, Abstract Art. The title of the Impressionist movement was taken from his *Impression: Sunrise*.

◆ see Pierre-Auguste Renoir p. 60

▲ *ABOVE:* Le Pont Japonais, Bassin aux Nympheas, *one of the many works of art that Monet painted in his garden at Giverny.*

MUNCH, EDVARD (1863–1944)

Munch studied in Christiania (now Oslo) and travelled in Germany, Italy and France before settling in Oslo. During his time in Paris (1908) he came under the influence of Gauguin and had immense sympathy for Van Gogh due to the bouts of mental illness from which both of them suffered. In fact, this would have a profound effect on the development of Munch as an artist and explains the extraordinary passion that pervades his work. Life, love and death are the themes that he endlessly explored in his paintings, rendered in an Expressionist symbolic style. His use of swirling lines and strident colours emphasize the angst that lies behind his paintings. He also produced etchings, lithographs and woodcut engravings which influenced the German artists of the movement known as Die Brücke.

see Claude Monet p. 50

NUREYEV, RUDOLF (1938–93)

Rudolf Hametovich Nureyev, born in Irkutsk, Siberia, in 1938, was the principal dancer at the famous Kirov Ballet until 1961. In that year, he defected to the West by leaping over a barrier at a Paris airport to elude his Soviet 'minders'. After claiming political asylum, he danced with important western ballet companies, including the Royal Ballet at Covent Garden, London, where he formed a highly successful partnership with Margot Fonteyn.

see Igor Stravinsky p. 73

ORWELL, GEORGE (1903–1950)

Eric Arthur Blair, better known by the pen-name George Orwell, was a British author best remembered today for two of his novels: *Animal Farm* (1945) and *Nineteen Eighty-Four* (1949). *Animal Farm* is ostensibly about a group of animals who oust the humans from the farm they live on and endeavour to run it themselves. It is an allegory about the events

▼ BELOW: Russian ballet dancer Rudolf Nureyev in a production of Le Corsaire in 1962.

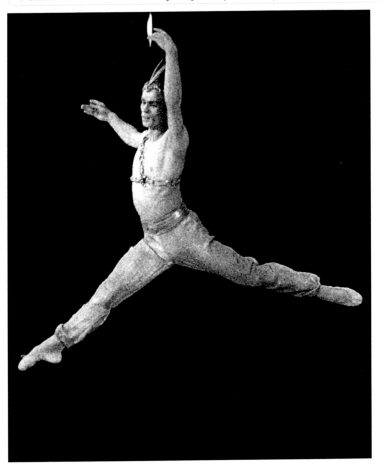

following the revolution in the Soviet Union, and in particular the rise of Stalinism. The world described in *Nineteen Eighty-Four* also has striking and deliberate parallels to Stalinist Russia – notably, the themes of a betrayed revolution and the subordination of individuals to 'the Party' and the extensive and institutional use of propaganda.

◘ *see* James Joyce p. 34

OWEN, WILFRED (1893–1918)

English poet, famous for his war poetry. Owen, who worked as a tutor before World War I, was invalided out in 1917 with shell shock. He was returned to the fighting in 1918 and killed seven days before the Armistice, on 4 November 1918. He was awarded the Military Cross. Most of Owen's poetry was not published until after his death, when his works were tirelessly lauded by his great friend and fellow poet, Siegfried Sassoon. His poems include 'Anthem for Doomed Youth' and 'Dulce et Decorum Est'.

◘ *see* T. E. Lawrence p. 39

PAVAROTTI, LUCIANO (b. 1935)

The beautiful voice of Italian tenor Luciano Pavarotti has been described as 'Sun-ripened in the warmth of Italy'. Originally a schoolteacher, Pavarotti turned to singing in 1961 and was immediately snapped up by the opera house in Reggio Emilia. He made his operatic debut as Rodolfo, the hero in Puccini's *La Bohème* and never looked back. He toured Europe with the famous La Scala Opera of Milan (1963–64) and in 1968 made his first appearance at New York's Metropolitan Opera House. Pavarotti has done much to popularize opera and in 1991 gave a mass concert – Pavarotti in the Park – in Hyde Park, London. He has appeared in the popular concerts given by the 'Three Tenors' – Pavarotti, Placido Domingo and José Carreras.

◘ *see* Placido Domingo p. 23

▲ ABOVE: *Italian tenor Luciano Pavarotti, who has done much to bring opera music to the wider public.*

PIAF, EDITH (1915–63)

French singer Piaf (her nickname, meaning 'sparrow'), is forever linked with her signature tune *Non, Je ne regrette rien*. Piaf performed on stage, film, television and radio and remains one of France's best-loved musicians.

◆ *see* Jeanne Moreau p. 118

PICASSO, PABLO (1881–1973)

Pablo Picasso was a sculptor, draughtsman and ceramicist, the most versatile and influential artist of the twentieth century. Having studied in Barcelona, Picasso finally settled in Paris in 1904. His Blue (1901–04) and Rose (1904–06) periods produced his popular scenes of vagrants and circus performers, which were loosely inspired by Puvis and the Symbolists. Then, in 1907, he produced *Les Demoiselles d'Avignon*, the most influential painting of the twentieth century. Named after the red-light district in Barcelona and drawing inspiration from African sculpture, it opened the way for the Cubist movement, which Picasso spearheaded with Braque.

In the 1920s he ushered in a Classical revival, while also being hailed as an inspiration by the Surrealists. Increasingly, though, his paintings displayed a pessimistic strain, brought on by the collapse of his marriage and the deteriorating political situation. This culminated in his most celebrated picture, *Guernica*, which commemorated an atrocity in the Spanish Civil War. Picasso's ongoing hostility to the Franco regime led him to make France, rather than Spain, the base for his later artistic activities.

◆ *see* Paul Cézanne p. 17

▶ *RIGHT: Spanish cubist painter and sculptor, Pablo Picasso.*

POLLOCK, JACKSON (1912–56)

Pollock grew up in the American West, becoming familiar with Native American art at an early age. He was briefly influenced by Benton and the Regionalists, but learned more from Siqueiros and the Mexican muralists. He was impressed by their expressive, almost violent use of paint. Pollock also began to explore the possibilities of Jungian psychology. This started as an aspect of his private life – psychotherapy was one of the many treatments he tried for his long-term alcoholism – but it also fuelled his art. For, like the Surrealists, he adopted the idea of automatic painting, as a mirror of the subconscious.

After years of isolation and critical neglect, Pollock's experiments bore fruit in the late 1940s. By 1947, he had perfected the 'drip' technique which made him famous. He placed his canvas on the floor and covered it in trails of paint, poured directly from the can. This process was carried out in an artistic frenzy, comparable with the Indian ritual dances which he had witnessed as a boy. Pollock's output slowed in the 1950s, and he was killed in a car crash in 1956.

■ see Sigmund Freud p. 274

PROUST, MARCEL (1871–1922)

French writer Marcel Proust originally studied law at the Sorbonne , but was already writing at this time and published his first works in 1896. He won the *Prix Goncourt* in 1919 with his first book, *A la Recherche du Temps Perdu* ('Remembrance of Things Past', 1913) – a unique and compelling psychoanalytical autobiography in several volumes.

■ see Jean-Paul Sartre p. 69

◄ *LEFT: Marcel Proust, author of* A la Recherche du Temps Perdu.

PULLMAN, PHILIP (b. 1946)

British writer Philip Pullman studied literature at Oxford and began writing for children while working as a teacher. Real success, however, came with the publication of the *His Dark Materials* trilogy – a fantasy series that caught the imagination of adults and children alike and has made Pullman one of the most popular writers of the twenty-first century.

◆ *see* J. K. Rowling p. 66

QUANT, MARY (b. 1934)

Mary Quant is an English fashion designer credited with inventing the miniskirt and hot pants. In October 1955, she opened a clothes shop on the Kings Road in London, England, called Bazaar, which became a popular haunt for the fashionable Chelsea Set of 'Swinging London'. Her skirts had been getting shorter since about 1958 – a development she considered to be practical and liberating, allowing women the ability to run for a bus. The miniskirt became one of the defining fashions of the 1960s. In 1966 Quant was appointed an OBE for services to the fashion industry. In the late 1960s, Quant launched hot pants, her last big fashion development.

◆ *see* Vivienne Westwood p. 76

RENOIR, PIERRE-AUGUSTE (1841–1919)

Renoir was a leading figure of the Impressionist style. He founded the movement with Claude Monet, based upon their developing a style of painting that attempted to capture the spirit of the subject by using a less precise and more evident brush-stroke. Unlike Monet, Renoir was at his best in the portrayal of figures, as can be seen in the *Bathers* (1887). Renoir particularly enjoyed scenes of middle-class French society and females, either nude or in movement. Renoir's palette was characteristically light, his technique almost gentle in its application, which gives his genre paintings an almost welcoming air, drawing the viewer into the scene.

◆ *see* Claude Monet p. 50

REGO, PAULA (b. 1935)

Rego was born in Lisbon, but her father worked for Marconi in Essex, and she was educated at an English school. In 1952, she entered the Slade School of Art, where she trained under Coldstream. There she met Victor Willing, a fellow painter, who became her husband in 1959. They lived in Portugal until 1963, after which they resided principally in England.

Rego's early work was strongly influenced by Dubuffet. She also produced semi-abstract collages, sometimes with political overtones. Increasingly, though, she turned to figurative painting, drawing much of her inspiration from children's illustration, nursery rhymes and her own memories of childhood. In mature works, such as *The Maids*, these playful elements are transposed into unsettling contexts, hinting at games of a very sinister kind. Rego's paintings have brought her success, both in Portugal and the UK. She has twice represented her native land at the Bienal in São Paolo, and on one occasion for Britain. In 1990, she became the first Associate Artist of the National Gallery in London.

◆ *see* Bridget Riley p. 61

RILEY, BRIDGET (b. 1931)

Bridget Riley studied at Goldsmith's College of Art (1949–52) and the Royal College of Art (1952–55) in London. She had her first one-woman exhibition at Gallery One, London, in 1962 and has had many other shows all over the world in subsequent years. Influenced by the Futurists Giacomo Balla and Umberto Boccioni, she began to develop an optical style in the 1960s – now known as Op Art – in which hallucinatory images were created in black and white, in geometric or curvilinear patterns endlessly repeated to produce the illusion of rippling or undulating movement. By 1966 she had moved into colour, which enabled her to widen the scope of these images considerably; her colours vary in depth and tone and add subtlety to the overall pattern. Widely acclaimed in England, she made an impact on the international scene in 1968 when she became the first British artist to win the top award for painting at the Venice Biennale.

see Paula Rego p. 61

RIVERA, DIEGO (1886–1957)

The outstanding muralist of Latin America, Diego Rivera studied art in Mexico City and Madrid; he went to Paris in 1911, where he met Picasso and began painting Cubist works, which were strongly influenced by Gris and Braque. By contrast, a sojourn in Italy studying the frescoes of the Renaissance Masters made such an impact on him that, on his return to Mexico in 1921, he concentrated on large murals decorating the walls of public buildings. These depicted every aspect of life in Mexico and drew on the turbulent history of its people. Rivera's best work was carried out during a period when Mexico was dominated by left-wing, anti-clerical governments, which regarded Rivera as the leading revolutionary artist. He also worked in the USA where he painted murals extolling the industrial proletariat and preaching social messages. He evolved his own brand of folk art with overtones of such disparate elements as Aztec symbolism and Byzantine icons.

see Frida Kahlo p. 37

▶ *RIGHT: British abstract painter Bridget Riley.*

RODIN, AUGUSTE (1840–1917)

French sculptor Rodin struggled for acceptance in his earlier career and was rejected by the Paris School of Arts several times. Following a visit to Italy to study the sculpture of his hero Michelangelo, Rodin's work took on a Classical, monumental appeal with his work *The Age of Bronze* (1877). The sculpture was so realistic that Rodin was accused of working from a cast. By the turn of the century Rodin was proclaimed by many as the greatest sculptor of the time. With renowned works such as *The Thinker* and *The Kiss,* the name Rodin has become inseparable from the medium of sculpture.

◖ *see* Alberto Giacometti p. 29

ROHE, LUDWIG MIES VAN DER (1886–1969)

Ludwig Mies van der Rohe was an architect and designer. Though born and trained in Germany, he fled reluctantly in the late 1930s as he saw the Nazis growing in power. When he arrived in the United States, he was already an influential designer. Van der Rohe settled in Chicago where he designed and built many modern high-rises in Chicago's downtown and elsewhere. Some of his credits include the Federal Building (1959), the IBM Building (1966) and 860–880 Lake Shore Drive (1948–52) – the first building to use an all glass and steel curtain wall in its construction, the hallmark of the modern skyscraper. In 1958 van der Rohe built what has been regarded as the ultimate expression of the International Style of architecture, the Seagram Building in New York. It is a large glass work, but controversially, van der Rohe chose to include a massive plaza and fountain in front of the structure, creating an open space in Park Avenue.

◖ *see* Le Corbusier p. 39

▶ *RIGHT: Auguste Rodin's* The Thinker *at Stanford University, California.*

ROTHKO, MARK (1903–70)

Born Marcus Rothkovitch in Dvinsk, Russia, Rothko emigrated to the US in 1913. He studied briefly at Yale and in New York, although he considered this to have had little influence on his painting. Rothko's style took many years to evolve. His early figurative works included portraits and psychologically-infused urban scenes, which he exhibited with the American expressionist group, The Ten. Rothko embraced ancient myth as he moved into a surrealist phase in the late 1930s, drawing on them as subjects for his increasingly abstract works. By 1946, he had moved into pure abstraction, painting amorphous shapes (or 'Multiforms') that would coalesce into his familiar rectangles on fields of colour by 1949. Although the works were formally quite simple, Rothko executed them with a meticulous eye for colour, balance and brushwork that give them a dramatic presence beyond their initial appearance. He was pleased that viewers often found looking at his paintings a deeply emotional experience. While he maintained the essential elements of his signature style, Rothko's paintings became generally larger, darker and more meditative in the last dozen years of his life.

see Salvador Dali p. 21

ROWLING, J. K. (b. 1965)

British writer J. K. Rowling shot to fame after the publication of her first book, *Harry Potter and the Philosopher's Stone*. This was just the first in an on-going series following the character of Harry Potter, a young boy who attends a school for wizards. The books have achieved phenomenal success and cult status amongst adults and children alike, and Rowling has been the recipient of several awards.

see J. R. R. Tolkien p. 74

RUSHDIE, SALMAN (b. 1947)

Author Salman Rushdie's most famous work is *The Satanic Verses* (1988) which, in part, portrayed the life of Muhammad. The book was condemned by sections of the Muslim community, banned in India and Rushdie received death threats. The controversy and furore surrounding its publication only served to increase interest in it, and it is now considered a seminal work of the late-twentieth century.

◆ *see* J. K. Rowling p. 66

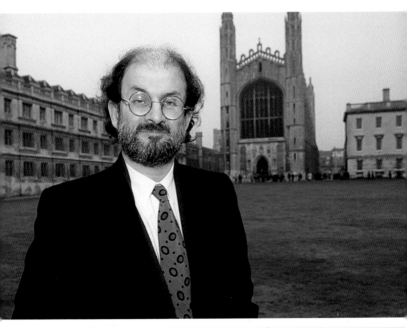

▲ *ABOVE: Controversial author Salman Rushdie.*

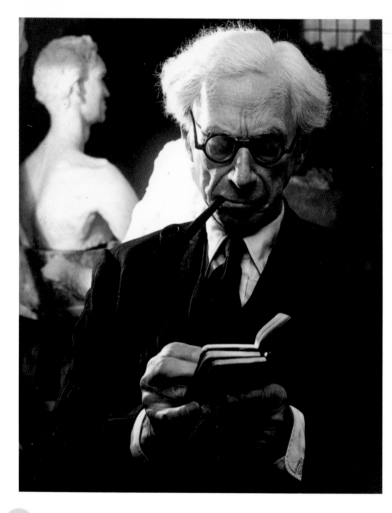

◀ *LEFT: Mathematician and philosopher Bertrand Russell.*

RUSSELL, BERTRAND (1872–1970)

The British mathematician and philosopher Bertrand Russell was educated at Cambridge, where his interests were first inspired. He wrote *Principles of Mathematics* (1903), *Problems of Philosophy* (1911) and *Principles of Social Reconstruction* (1917). His *Introduction to Mathematical Philosophy* (1919) was written while the author imprisoned for pacifist writings, *Marriage and Morals* (1929), *An Enquiry into Meaning and Truth* (1940), *History of Western Philosophy* (1946) and *New Hopes for a Changing World* (1951). He was awarded the Order of Merit in 1949 and the Nobel Prize for Literature in 1950.

◆ *see* Jean-Paul Sartre p. 69

SARTRE, JEAN-PAUL (1905–80)

After wartime service in the Resistance during the German occupation of his country, the French philosopher and writer Jean-Paul Sartre became a hero of the French Left, alongside his partner the feminist Simone de Beauvoir (1908–86). Between them they represented intellectual Paris's dominant presence. In philosophical works like *Being and Nothingness* (1943) as well as in a string of well-regarded novels and plays, he became the figurehead for the then-fashionable philosophy of Existentialism. An atheist, he argued that, in a cosmos without a creator, the individual had to make his own way, without reliance on religious or other props. (*See over for illustration.*)

◆ *see* Bertrand Russell p. 69

▲ ABOVE: French philosopher Jean-Paul Sartre.

SCHOENBERG, ARNOLD (1874–1951)

Together with Igor Stravinsky, Schoenberg has become the most influential figure in twentieth-century classical music. In his youth he wrote music in a ripe and sumptuously orchestrated late-Romantic style, but came to believe that the later music of Wagner, and that of Mahler and Strauss, as well as his own, was undermining the great tradition from which it sprang: the Austro-German tonal tradition in which a sense of key and of tensions between the keys is structurally crucial. He at first resolved to accept this development as inevitable and necessary. He found, however, that this atonal music could not generate the powerfully logical forms that had made tonal music so durable, and over a period, devised the 12-note system to replace them. His music was slow to achieve acceptance, and he was regarded as dangerously destructive.

⬥ *see* Igor Stravinsky p. 73

SHAW, GEORGE BERNARD (1856–1950)

Born in Dublin in 1856, Shaw later moved to London to embark on a writing career. Between 1879 and 1883 he produced five novels, all of which were rejected by publishers, so he became a music and drama critic and made an impact with his trenchant views and sometimes acerbic comments in the *Saturday Review*. After 1882, when he encountered the works of Karl Marx, Shaw became a Socialist and two years later joined the Fabian Society. In 1885, Shaw finally embarked on the writing career that ensured his fame and reputation – as a dramatist. His first play was Widowers' Houses, and this was followed by *Mrs Warren's Profession* (1898), *Arms and the Man* (1898), *Major Barbara* (1905), *Pygmalion* (1913) – which was adapted as the musical *My Fair Lady* in 1956 – and several others that were infused with his socialist ideas. Shaw became particularly well known for his skilful depiction of female characters, but he also fell foul of the censors for some of his more controversial political and social arguments. He was awarded the Nobel Prize for Literature in 1925.

◆ see T. S. Eliot p. 25

SOUTINE, CHAIM (1894–1943)

Born at Smilovich, Russian Poland (now Belarus), Chaim Soutine studied in Vilnius and travelled to Paris in 1911, where he was befriended by fellow Russian Jew Marc Chagall. Modigliani introduced him to the Expressionist school in Paris and he, in turn, exerted an exotic influence on its development, adding a dash of Fauvism and the German approach to Expressionism. Soutine delighted in painting the carcasses of animals, much to the disgust and annoyance of neighbours, who habitually complained of the stench of rotting flesh that emanated from his studio. Apart from studies of dead birds and decomposing sides of beef, Soutine painted portraits whose emaciated features and deathly expression bear a gruesome resemblance to the living dead of Belsen and Auschwitz. Soutine, who continued to live in Paris after the fall of France, managed to evade deportation to the camps and died in Paris in 1943.

◆ see Amadeo Modigliani p. 49

SPENCER, SIR STANLEY (1891–1959)

Stanley Spencer spent most of his life in the village of Cookham, which provided him with most of his inspiration. He studied at the Slade School of Art in London from 1909 to 1912 but appears not to have been affected by any of the avant-garde developments in that period. Apart from military service in World War I, and a period during World War II spent on Clydeside recording the toil of shipyards, he remained very close to his roots – a familiar sight in Cookham, painting or sketching. Often dismissed as an eccentric, he worked outside the artistic mainstream, but inevitably some trends in art found a reflection in his paintings, notably his use of distorted anatomy and space. A profoundly religious man, his paintings often have biblical connotations, although events such as the Resurrection are placed in the context of Cookham or Clydeside. He covered his enormous canvasses with drawings of the subjects, which were then painted over. He was knighted shortly before he died.

◆ *see* Francis Bacon p. 12

STRAVINSKY, IGOR (1882–1971)

One of the most distinguished composers of the twentieth century, the Russian Igor Stravinsky came to eminence and international acclaim with his ballets *The Firebird* and *Petrushka*. By 1913 Stravinsky developed the challenging technique of polytonality (the use of numerous keys at the same time). In his later works, such as *Orpheus,* Stravinsky turned to a Neoclassical style. It is for the seminal – and much-critically-discussed – *Rite of Spring*, however, that Starvinksy is best-remembered. The piece's dissonance, lack of melodic key and juxtaposed musical sections had people walking out of the premiere in 1913, although it has since become one of the most lauded classical pieces of the twentieth century.

◆ *see* Arnold Schoenberg p. 71

TIPPETT, SIR MICHAEL (1905–98)

English composer Michael Tippett's open receptivity to a myriad of cultures and musical styles made hhim one of the most profoundly communicative composers of the twentieth century. His left-wing politics were to surface many times in his music and were of central importance in his life. One of the most fascinating aspects of his music is the belief in the principle of Austro-German music, particularly Beethoven. Alongside this lies a deep interest in Early English music. The choral works *A Child of Our Time* (1939–41) and *The Mask of Time* (1980–82) and his operas all explore Tippett's social and human preoccupations.

◆ *see* Philip Glass p. 32

TOLKIEN, J. R. R. (1892–1973)

English author J. R. R. Tolkien was born in South Africa but his family returned to England while he was still a child. Throughout his early years he cultivated a love of ancient languages and studied philology at Oxford. This fascination became evident in many of his works, in which he invented his own languages such as the elvish tongue. Tolkien wrote *The Hobbit* in 1936 and it became an immediate best-seller. Shortly

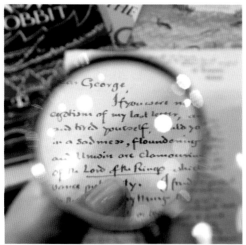

afterwards he began work on the sequel – this time, though, it was written with an adult audience in mind. *The Lord of the Rings* took more than a decade to write and was eventually published in three volumes. It remains one of the most popular works of fiction of all time.

◆ *see* J. K. Rowling p. 66

▲ *ABOVE: Works and letters by J. R. R. Tolkien.*

TOLSTOY, COUNT LEO (1828–1910)

The Russian novelist and philosopher Leo Tolstoy was one of the literary giants of our time and his two epic novels *War and Peace* (1865–69) and *Anna Karenina* (1875–77) have become hallmarks of literature. Tolstoy wrote during a turbulent time in Russian history, which is reflected in his profound, brilliantly written, morally aware novels. Serving in the Russian army during the Crimean War, Tolstoy later became a pacifist and rejected the domineering religion of Russia.

◆ *see* Bertrand Russell p. 69

WARHOL, ANDY (1928–87)

Warhol was born in Pittsburgh, the son of Czech immigrants. In 1949 he moved to New York, where he became a successful commercial artist. This gave him a solid grounding in silkscreen printing techniques and taught him the value of self-promotion – both of which were to feature heavily in his art. Warhol's breakthrough came when he began to make paintings of familiar, everyday objects, such as soup cans, dollar bills and brillo pads. Early examples were hand-painted, but Warhol soon decided to use mechanical processes as far as possible. His aim, in this respect, was to free the image from any connotations of craftsmanship, aesthetics or individuality. He further emphasized this by describing his studio as 'The Factory'.

Warhol rapidly extended his references to popular culture by portraying celebrities (Marilyn Monroe, Marlon Brando), as well as more sinister items, such as news clippings with car crashes or the electric chair. He also associated himself with other branches of the mass media, notably through his links with the rock band The Velvet Underground, and through his controversial films.

◆ *see* Roy Lichtenstein p. 39

WELLES, ORSON (1915–85)

Welles' career was dominated by his legendary film *Citizen Kane* (1941).
He co-wrote, directed and starred in movie, which is now considered by
many to be one of the most formative films ever made.

◆ *see* George Orwell p. 52

WESTWOOD, VIVIENNE (b. 1941)

Vivienne Westwood is an English fashion designer largely responsible for
modern punk and new-wave fashions. She is linked with the Sex Pistols
via Malcolm McLaren and their 'Sex' boutique on Kings Road, Chelsea in
London during the 1960s. In December 2003, she and the Wedgwood
pottery company launched a series of tea sets featuring her designs.

◆ *see* Malcolm Mclaren p. 45

WILLIAMS, JOHN (b. 1932)

American composer John William's early work as a studio pianist in
Hollywood led to pockets of work in the early 1960s. During the 1970s
he produced music for a number of films including *The Towering Inferno*
(1974). Following collaborations with Steven Spielberg in the mid-1970s,
Williams wrote the music to *Star Wars* (1977). He adopts music from a
wide variety of genres and has worked hard to prove his credentials as a
serious composer. It is in the dramatic mainstream, however, that he has
proved most successful.

◆ *see* Steven Spielberg p. 128

WILSON, JACQUELINE (b. 1945)

Jacqueline Wilson has sold over eight million copies of her books in the
UK alone and they have been translated into 23 different languages. Her
work is so popular with children because she does not talk down to

them and her characters and their situations are realistic. Her work has dealt with themes such as having to deal with divorced parents and first-time adult relationships. Wilson has been on countless shortlists and has won several awards, including The Young Telegraph/Fully Booked Award for *The Bed and Breakfast Star* (1995), and the Children's Book of the Year and the Guardian Children's Fiction Award for *The Illustrated Mum* (1999).

◆ *see* J. K. Rowling p. 66

WRIGHT, FRANK LLOYD (1869–1959)

American architect Frank Lloyd Wright was studying engineering at Wisconsin University when the newly built wing of the Wisconsin State Capitol collapsed. Wright decided to turn to architecture instead, but to use engineering principles to ensure safe designs. One of his innovations was to 'build low', constructing prairie-style bungalows. Between 1916 and 1920, Wright built the steel and concrete Imperial Hotel in Tokyo, Japan: three years later, the Hotel survived a massive earthquake measuring around eight on the Richter scale. Considered one of the greatest of twentieth-century architects, Frank Lloyd Wright was a devotee of Cubist spatial ideas and open planning. Wright's best-known work was design for the Guggenheim Museum of Art (1959) in New York in which the exhibits line the walls of a continuous spiral ramp.

◆ *see* Antonio Gaudi p. 28

YASUNARI, KAWABATA (1899–1972)

Distinguished Japanese writer Kawabata Yasunari wrote *The Izu Dancer* (1925) combining the literary impact of Surrealism and Dadaism while also retaining Japanese traditions. Yasunari won the Nobel Prize in 1968.

◆ *see* Salvador Dalí p. 21

POPULAR ENTERTAINMENT

1937	Walt Disney's *Snow White and the Seven Dwarfs* becomes the first feature-length animation
1939	Clark Gable and Vivienne Leigh star in *Gone With the Wind*
1943	Humphrey Bogart stars in *Casablanca*
1946	Cary Grant stars in the Hitchcock thriller *Notorious*
1953	Marilyn Monroe stars in *Gentlemen Prefer Blondes*
1955	James Dean is killed in a car crash
1956	The Beatles are formed
1959	Buddy Holly is killed in a plane crash
1961	Audrey Hepburn stars in *Breakfast at Tiffany's*
1962	The Rolling Stones are formed
1969	Jimi Hendrix plays the Woodstock festival
1971	Elton John releases 'Your Song'
1977	Steven Spielberg releases the first *Star Wars* film; Elvis Presley dies; Charlie Chaplin dies
1980	Robert de Niro stars in *Raging Bull*
1985	Bob Geldof organizes Live Aid
1986	Tom Cruise stars in *Top Gun*
1987	Fred Astaire dies; Sean Connery wins an Oscar for *The Untouchables*
1991	Freddie Mercury dies of AIDS
1993	Quentin Tarantino makes *Reservoir Dogs*
1994	Woody Allen directs *Bullets Over Broadway*; Kurt Cobain commits suicide
2000	Madonna releases her album *Music*

ALLEN, WOODY (b. 1935)

Allen is an American independent film director and writer who stars in many of his films. His work is filled with persistent themes of religion, relationships and society – Allen's society being confined largely to a cultural 'high society' in New York. Among his 30-plus films are *Annie Hall* (1977), *Hannah and her Sisters* (1986) and *Bullets Over Broadway* (1994).

see Alfred Hitchcock p. 104

ASTAIRE, FRED (1899–1987)

Born in Nebraska, USA, Astaire went to Hollywood in 1933 and found fame as a film actor/dancer, depite an unpromising start when a screen test noted him as 'Can't sing. Can't act. Slightly balding. Can dance a bit'. He is most notably associated with dance partner Ginger Rogers, with whom he was prominent in the emerging genre of musical films during the 1930s and 40s. he later gave up dancing, but still took movie roles in films such as *On the Beach* (1959) and *The Towering Inferno* (1974).

see Ginger Rogers p. 123

BARDOT, BRIGITTE (b. 1934)

French model-turned-actress, Bardot was made an international sex symbol in the 1956 film by Roger Vadim (her first husband) *And God Created Woman*. She was one of the few European actresses at the time to be hailed by Hollywood as a glamour icon. She retired from film in the 1970s to concentrate on campaigning for animal rights.

see Marilyn Monroe p. 115

▲ ABOVE: International model and star of the big screen, Brigitte Bardot.

80

BEATLES, THE (1956)

Paul McCartney (bass guitar), John Lennon (rhythm guitar), Ringo Starr (drums) and George Harrison (guitar) formed The Beatles in Liverpool (*c.* 1956). With the formidable songwriting team of Lennon and McCartney, The Beatles were arguably the most influential band of the twentieth century. Their phenomenally successful music was guitar-orientated, with an emphasis on vocal harmonies. Their 'concept album' *Sergeant Pepper's Lonely Hearts Club Band* (1967) was particularly influential. The band also made several films, including *Help!* (1965). The group disbanded in 1970.

see John Lennon p. 108, Paul McCartney p. 112

▼ BELOW: *Perhaps one of the most well-known images of The Beatles, the famous foursome on the cover of their hit album,* Abbey Road.

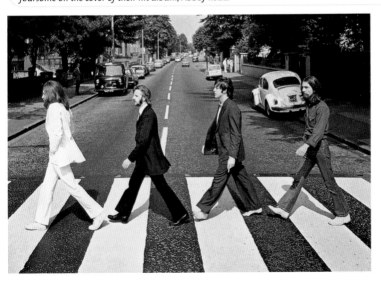

BERGMAN, INGRID (1915–82)

When still very young, Ingrid Bergman lost both her parents and was raised by relatives. She studied at the Royal Dramatic Theater in Stockholm and her first screen appearance was in the little-known *Munkbrogreven* (1934). After a dozen or so Swedish films, she went to the USA and appeared in *Intermezzo* (1939), which brought her to public attention. Arguably her most famous part was in *Casablanca* (1942), playing opposite Humphrey Bogart. In the 1950s she met Roberto Rossellini, and became his mistress during the making of *Stromboli* (1950), in which she starred. At the time they were both married to other people, and their affair became a scandal. When she had a baby with Rossellini, she was described as 'Hollywood's apostle of degradation'. It was with *Anastasia* (1956), that she regained her star status and her performance in Ingmar Bergman's *Autumn Sonata* (1978) was acclaimed as her finest hour.

◆ *see* Isabella Rossellini p. 123

BOGARDE, SIR DIRK (1921–99)

English actor Dirk Bogarde became a household name playing a doctor in a series of 1950s films and later won critical acclaim for his skilful portrayal of evil in *The Servant* (1963).

◆ *see* Richard Burton p. 84

BOGART, HUMPHREY (1899–1957)

An icon of film, American actor Humphrey Bogart starred in many enduring 1940s and 50s films, including *Casablanca* (1943) with Ingrid Bergman, *The African Queen* (1951) with Katharine Hepburn and *The Big Sleep* with his fourth wife, Lauren Bacall.

◆ *see* Katharine Hepburn p. 104

BOWIE, DAVID (b. 1947)

David Robert Jones, better known as David Bowie, first came to public attention when his single 'Space Oddity' was released to coincide with the Moon landing in 1969, but it did not become a UK hit record until later. *Hunky Dory* (1971) was a far more successful record which reveals some of his influences – 'Song for Bob Dylan' and 'Andy Warhol'. In an 18-month period in 1972 and 1973 he had four top-ten albums and eight top-ten singles in the UK. One of these was the seminal *The Rise and Fall of Ziggy Stardust and the Spiders from Mars* – a concept album relating the career of an extraterrestrial rock singer. In the 1980s, Bowie did an about-face and made an unabashed bid for commercial success, which he achieved with *Let's Dance* (1983). In 2003, he was reported to be the second-richest entertainer in the UK (behind Paul McCartney), with an estimated fortune of £510 million.

◆ *see* Paul McCartney p. 112

BRANDO, MARLON (b. 1924)

Regard for US actor Brando, like his career, is erratic. He is best known for his early role in *On the Waterfront* (1954) and latterly as Don Corleone in *The Godfather* (1972). Despite his somewhat erratic career, Brando was to prove a huge influence on the younger generation of actors, including James Dean.

◆ *see* James Dean p. 89

BROWN, JAMES (b. 1928)

While some say Macon, Georgia, USA, it is generally believed that James Brown was born in Barnwell, South Carolina. As a teenager from an impoverished background, he turned to petty crime and was eventually sent to prison. But having secured an early release, he turned his considerable energies to music. Brown's innovations in funk music have been extraordinarily influential. In the late 1960s and early 1970s, his irresistible sound spawned countless imitators. With the advent of hip hop in the late 1970s, Brown's grooves became the foundation for rap music and breakdancing. In the late 1980s, Brown's music experienced a renaissance with the rise of sampling by hip-hop producers. Snippets of his songs were recycled into hundreds of rap songs.

■ see Jimi Hendrix p. 102

BURTON, RICHARD (1925–84)

Welsh-born actor Richard Burton made a successful transition to Hollywood in the early 1950s, where he achieved fame equally for his reputation as a fast-living heavy drinker and his relationship with Elizabeth Taylor (one of five wives he eventually took) as he did for impressive acting in films such as *Who's Afraid of Virginia Woolf?* (1966).

■ see Elizabeth Taylor p. 130

CAGNEY, JAMES (1899–1986)

Born in a tough area of New York, actor James Cagney drew on his early experiences to achieve great acclaim with his roles as a troubled gangster in classic films such as *Public Enemy* (1931) and *Angels with Dirty Faces* (1938).

■ see Clint Eastwood p. 97

CAINE, MICHAEL (b. 1933)

English actor Michael Caine established himself in the world of film in the 1960s by playing working-class characters such as the infamous *Alfie* (1966). Occasionally the target for criticism for his unchanging (some say wooden) acting style, Caine has recently earned praise with films such as *Little Voice* (1998).

■ see Sean Connery p. 87

CHAN, JACKIE (b. 1954)

Jackie Chan, born Chan Kong, is a Hong Kong martial artist, actor, director and stuntman. He is the star of over 100 Kung Fu movies, known for his comic, acrobatic fighting style and use of improvised weapons. In his biography, Chan says he created his screen persona as a reaction to that of Bruce Lee. Where Lee's characters were typically stern, morally upright heroes, Chan plays well-meaning, slightly foolish guys who triumph in the end. Chan's appearances in films like *Battle Creek Brawl* (1980), *Cannonball Run* (1980) and *Cannonball Run II* (1984) gained him a certain cult following in the US, but it was *Rumble in the Bronx* (1995) that gave him his break into the mainstream.

◆ *see* Bruce Lee p. 107

CHAPLIN, CHARLIE (1889–1977)

South-London-born Charlie Chaplin became one of the brightest stars of the silent cinema in his unforgettable persona – half-hilarious, half-melancholy – of the bowler-hatted, cane-wielding, splay-footed 'tramp'. A co-founder of the United Artists' studio, aimed at giving creative actors more control over their work, he directed several classic films, including the scathing social satire, *Modern Times*. His films bridged the gap between humour and pathos. (*See over for illustration.*)

◆ *see* Stan Laurel and Oliver Hardy p. 107

CLEESE, JOHN (b. 1939)

Born in Weston-super-Mare in the county of Somerset, England, John Cleese's talent for comedy emerged as a member of the Cambridge Footlights Revue during the time that he was a law student at Downing College. He became famous as one of the members of the *Monty Python*

"Charlie"

team, his most memorable moments being in the 'Cheese Shop', 'Ministry of Silly Walks' and 'Dead Parrot' sketches. Later he appeared as the awful hotel manager Basil Fawlty in the television series *Fawlty Towers*, which he also co-wrote with then-wife Connie Booth.

◆ *see* Michael Palin p. 120

COBAIN, KURT (1967–1994)

Kurt Cobain was the lead singer of the cult band Nirvana, the other members of which were Dave Grohl and Krist Novoselic. Cobain was highly influential in creating and popularizing what came to be termed 'grunge music' – a style that evolved as a reaction against the perceived superficiality of 1980s stadium rock and over-the-top metal bands with preened images and elaborate stage shows. He is best known for the song 'Smells Like Teen Spirit' (1991). He also wrote a song, 'Lithium', about the medication lithium carbonate, which is used to treat bipolar disorder. Cobain, depressed and in a heroin-induced haze, committed suicide at the age of 27 with a shotgun blast in his mouth.

◆ *see* Jimi Hendrix p. 102

CONNERY, SEAN (b. 1930)

Scottish actor Sean Connery was most famous for his portrayal of the quintessential English spy James Bond in his early years. He starred as 007 six times before retiring from the role in 1971 after *Diamonds are Forever*. He has continued to make quality films since then, however, and he received an Oscar for his part in the *The Untouchables* in 1987.

◆ *see* Roger Moore p. 115

◀ LEFT: Charlie Chaplin, one of the world's best-loved comedians, in his classic 'disguise'.

COPPOLA, FRANCIS FORD (b. 1939)

Francis Ford Coppola made his name as a filmmaker in the 1970s as the co-writer and director of *The Godfather* (1971). The movie was an enormous box-office hit, smashing previous records to become the highest-grossing film of all time (until that record was surpassed by *Jaws* in 1975). *The Godfather* and *The Godfather Part II* (1974) both won the Academy Award for Best Picture, the latter being the first sequel to do so. Following their success he set about filming *Apocalypse Now* (1979), loosely based on Joseph Conrad's *Heart of Darkness* and set during the Vietnam War. The film was beset by numerous problems, including typhoons, drug abuse and nervous breakdowns, and was delayed so often it was nicknamed 'Apocalypse Whenever'. When it was finally released, the film was equally lauded and hated by critics. After a lengthy break, Coppola returned to directing, with some commercial and critical success. *The Godfather Part III*, the third instalment in the *Godfather* saga, appeared in 1990.

Coppola's daughter Sofia is also a filmmaker and the first female director to receive the Academy Award, for *Lost In Translation* (2003).

◆ *see* Robert De Niro p. 89

CRAWFORD, JOAN (1904–77)

American actress Joan Crawford was renowned for her fiercely strong, often embittered female leads in the earlier years of cinema. Crawford's reputation unfortunately became bound to these harsh roles by a negative portrayal in her daughter's biography as an overbearing mother, and her earlier marriage to the actor Douglas Fairbanks, Jr, which ended when Fairbanks could no longer tolerate his wife's harsh ambition.

◆ *see* Bette Davis p. 89

CRUISE, TOM (b. 1962)

American actor Tom Cruise's star status was secured with the 1986 film *Top Gun*, which remains a perennial favourite for Cruise fans. Reputed to be a committed actor, Cruise has gained much respect for roles in films such as *Rain Man* (1988,) in which he played a hard-bitten young man who finds his autistic brother, and *Magnolia* (2000). He is known to embrace a wide variety of challenging roles. He was married for several years to the actress Nicole Kidman.

■ *see* Leonardo DiCaprio p. 93

DAVIS, BETTE (1908–89)

US actress Bette Davis is best known for her melodramatic starring roles in films such as *Jezebel* (1938) and, most famously, alongside Joan Crawford in *What Ever Happened to Baby Jane?* (1962).

■ *see* Joan Crawford p. 88

DE NIRO, ROBERT (b. 1943)

American actor Robert De Niro is renowned for his use of method acting, as evinced in the 1980 film *Raging Bull*. After a successful run in the 1970s, including acclaimed performances in *The Godfather Part II* (1974) and *Taxi Driver* (1976), there was a quiet period. De Niro's career was rejuvenated in the late 1980s by *The Untouchables* (1987) and he continues to turn in world-class performances. De Niro is one of America's most accomplished film actors.

■ *see* Francis Ford Coppola p. 88

DEAN, JAMES (1931–55)

A cinematic icon, Dean's early death preserved his image as an out-standing actor. Dean starred in only three films: *Rebel Without a Cause*

(1955), *East of Eden* (1955) and *Giant* (1956), the last two released after his death. Dean was as well known for his attitude as a troubled teenager (perhaps stemming from his mother's death when he was just a child), as for his burgeoning acting talent.

> *see* Marlon Brando p. 83

DENCH, JUDI (b. 1934)

Although ostensibly a stage and television actress, Dame Judi Dench has achieved both success and acclaim with her few film roles, most notably for her portrayal of Queen Victoria in the 1997 film *Mrs Brown* and her brief but much-lauded role as Queen Elizabeth I in the romantic comedy *Shakespeare in Love* (1998).

> *see* Sir Alec Guinness p. 102

DEPARDIEU, GERARD (b. 1948)

French actor Gerard Depardieu has realized a versatile and prolific career in French cinema and has broadened his horizons by breaking into Hollywood. He won much international acclaim with his 1989 film *Cyrano de Bergerac*.

> *see* Brigitte Bardot p. 80

DEPP, JOHNNY (b. 1963)

Born John Christopher Depp in Owensboro, Kentucky, USA, and raised in Florida, he dropped out of school at the age of 17 in hopes of becoming a rock musician. Depp discovered acting during a visit to LA with his former wife, who introduced him to actor Nicolas Cage. He made his film debut in *A Nightmare on Elm Street* (1984). In 1987, he shot to fame when

▶ RIGHT: Dame Judi Dench, Britain's best-loved stage and screen actress.

he replaced Jeff Yagher in the role of undercover cop Tommy Hanson in the popular TV series *21 Jump Street*. After numerous roles in teen films, his first of a few great collaborations with director Tim Burton came about when he portrayed the title role in *Edward Scissorhands* (1990). Following the film's success, Depp carved a niche for himself as a serious, somewhat dark, idiosyncratic performer.

◆ *see* Leonardo DiCaprio p. 93

DICAPRIO, LEONARDO (b. 1974)

The undisputed leader of the latest Hollywood 'Brat Pack', DiCaprio first came to attention for his impressive performance as a mentally handicapped boy, opposite Johnny Depp's lead, in *What's Eating Gilbert Grape* (1993). he rocketed to stardom and became the darling of the movie world because of his cherubic good looks and wild behaviour. He won the leading role in the multi-award-winning *Titanic* (1997) and Baz Luhrman's imaginative *Romeo and Juliet* (1996).

◆ *see* Johnny Depp p. 91

DIETRICH, MARLENE (1901–92)

Marlene Dietrich was a German-born film actress who possessed an ethereal quality, often playing lamentably ill-fated women. Among her acclaimed films are *Witness for the Prosecution* (1957) and *Morocco* (1930). She had a reputation for seducing her co-stars. She had a later career as a singer and performer, but eventually succumbed to alcoholism and spent the last few years of her life in seclusion.

◆ *see* Brigette Bardot p. 80

◀ *LEFT: The enigmatic, sensual Marlene Dietrich.*

DISNEY, WALT (1901–66)

Walter Elias Disney, Chicago-born creator of Mickey Mouse, worked for several years as a commercial artist before setting up his own animation studio. Mickey was in fact there from the beginning, in Disney's first independently produced films *Plane Crazy* and *Steamboat Willie* (both 1928). Made in 1937, *Snow White and the Seven Dwarfs* initiated an entirely new cinematic genre – the feature-length cartoon; it was followed by a long series of classics, including *Fantasia* (1940), *Dumbo* (1941) and *Bambi* (1942).

In the decades that followed, Disney and his corporation populated the consciousness of the world with a host of unforgettable characters: the original Disneyland theme park, opened in 1955, was Disney's personal brainchild.

◘ *see* Bart Simpson p. 126

DYLAN, BOB (b. 1941)

US singer/songwriter Bob Dylan was largely responsible for reviving the folk-song genre in the 1950s and 1960s. His songs, such as 'Blowin' in the Wind' (1962), were also key in the protest movement of that era. Although he is now inextricably identified with the era that he helped to define in his music, he has continued to impress younger generations with his musical abilities and people still flock to see his live performances. He remains one of the music industry's longest-standing veterans of the old style. (*See over for illustration.*)

◘ *see* The Beatles p. 81

◀ LEFT: Minnie Mouse at Eurodisney, the European equivalent of Walt Disney's brainchild, the Disneyland theme park.

EASTWOOD, CLINT (b. 1930)

Following success in television's *Rawhide*, Clint Eastwood's film career took off with Sergio Leones' 'spaghetti westerns' in the 1960s. Eastwood has admirably tackled the dual star/director role for several films, most notably *The Unforgiven* (1989). He is renowned for his minimalist style of acting.

see James Cagney p. 84

FLYNN, ERROL (1909–59)

Errol Flynn was born in Hobart, Tasmania, Australia. His acting career was unplanned, but with his very first film, *Captain Blood* (1935), he became a star. He was typecast as a swashbuckler and made appearances in the same vein in *The Adventures of Robin Hood* (1938), *The Sea Hawk* (1940) and *The Adventures of Don Juan* (1949). He had a reputation as a womanizer and was well known for having wild parties. By the mid 1950s, he was something of a self-parody but still won some acclaim as a drunken ne'er-do-well in *The Sun Also Rises* (1957). His autobiography, *My Wicked, Wicked Ways*, was published just months after his death from alcoholism and contains humorous anecdotes about Hollywood.

see Humphrey Bogart p. 82

FORD, HARRISON (b. 1942)

Harrison Ford was born in Chicago, Illinois, USA. He went to Hollywood to work as a carpenter before he broke through in movies. His first major role was in *American Graffiti* (1973). He went on to star as Han Solo in the

◀ LEFT: The singer-songwriter Bob Dylan is an icon for the 60s generation.

Star Wars trilogy. He starred in the title role of the *Indiana Jones* trilogy and as Jack Ryan in Tom Clancy's *Patriot Games* and *Clear and Present Danger*. For his performance in *Witness* (1985) he was nominated for an Oscar for Best Actor. His list of credits is impressive and he has appeared in four of the top-ten highest-grossing movies ever. Unsurprisingly then, he is reported to be the richest actor alive. In 2003, he received his star on Hollywood Boulevard.

◻ *see* Steven Spielberg p. 128

FOSTER, JODIE (b. 1962)

Double Oscar winner Jodie Foster has been acting in films since she was ten years old. Her most accomplished roles are in *Taxi Driver* (1976), *The Accused* (1988) and *The Silence of the Lambs* (1991).

◻ *see* Francis Ford Coppola p. 88

GABLE, CLARK (1901–60)

The souave star of over 60 films, American actor Clark Gable is best remembered as Rhett Butler in *Gone with the Wind* (1939). He died of a heart attack shortly after filming alongside Marilyn Monroe in *The Misfits*.

◻ *see* Marilyn Monroe p. 115

GARBO, GRETA (1905–90)

The Swedish-born film actress Greta Garbo made ten silent movies before her first 'talkie' in 1930 (*Anna Christie*), which made her an international star. After 13 further films, Garbo retired at the early age of 36. She was one of the most glamorous icons of the eraly film era.

◻ *see* Audrey Hepburn p. 103

▶ *RIGHT: The Swedish actress Greta Garbo.*

GARLAND, JUDY (1922–69)

American actress and singer Judy Garland made her stage premiere at the tender age of three. Her most famous role was as Dorothy in *The Wizard of Oz* (1939) but she also won great acclaim in *A Star is Born* (1954).

⬦ *see* Jodie Foster p. 98

GELDOF, BOB (b. 1951)

Bob Geldof first came to fame in the mid-1970s as leader of the Boomtown Rats, a rock group closely linked with the punk movement. In November 1984 Geldof saw a BBC news report on the famine in Ethiopia. He was so moved that he formed a group of leading rock musicians, called it Band Aid and, with Midge Ure from the band Ultravox, co-wrote the song, 'Do They Know It's Christmas'. The single was released just before Christmas with the aim of raising money for famine relief. Not content with the enormous success of the single, Geldof went on to organize Live Aid, a multi-venue rock-music concert held on 13 July 1985, which raised unprecedented sums for charity. He was nominated for the Nobel Peace Prize and received an honorary knighthood from Queen Elizabeth II.

⬦ *see* Elton John p. 106

GIBSON, MEL (b. 1956)

Mel Gibson was born in Peekskill, New York, one of 11 children, but was raised in Australia from the age of 12. Gibson's acting career began in Australia with appearances in the television series *The Sullivans*. He made his Australian film debut as the leather-clad, post-apocalyptic survivor in *Mad Max* (1979), which later became a cult hit and launched a series of films. In 1984 he made his US movie debut in *The Bounty*. Since then, Gibson has appeared in roles as diverse as maverick cop in the popular *Lethal Weapon* series and tortured prince in *Hamlet* (1990). He has had success behind the camera as well, receiving two Academy Awards (Best Director and Best Picture) for *Braveheart* (1995). His most recent is his most ambitious work, *The Passion of the Christ* (2004), a film in Aramaic, Hebrew and Latin.

◀ *see* Johnny Depp p. 90

GRANT, CARY (1904–86)

English-born actor Cary Grant combined sophisticated charm with impeccable delivery to comic roles, earning him a reputation as one of the most talented and sought-after actors of his generation. He played the romantic lead in films such as *Bringing up Baby* (1937). He expanded his genre later in his career, working with Alfred Hitchcock in tense thrillers such as *Notorious* (1946).

◀ *see* Alfred Hitchcock p. 104

▶ *RIGHT: Cary Grant.*

GUINNESS, SIR ALEC (1914–2000)

English actor Alec Guiness was a key figure in the Ealing Comedies of the 1940s and 50s. He was highly respected with an intensely reflective screen presence, noted in films such as *The Swan* (1956) and *Oliver Twist* (1948). A subtle and extremely versatile actor, Guinness was awarded an Oscar for *Bridge on the River Kwai* in 1958 – the same year he received his knighthood.

⬟ *see* Sir Laurence Olivier p. 119

HENDRIX, JIMI (1942–70)

The recordings of James Marshall 'Jimi' Hendrix during the psychedelic era redefined the sound of the electric guitar. He was as famous for his wild-man image and musical gimmickry as his music, such as burning and smashing his guitars on stage and appearing to play guitar with his teeth. With his band, The Jimi Hendrix Experience, he recorded anthems such as 'Hey Joe' and 'Purple Haze', whose heavily distorted guitar sound would be highly influential for the next 20 years. In August 1969 Hendrix, with a new band, played the Woodstock festival. The set featured an improvised, instrumental version of 'The Star-Spangled Banner', distorted almost beyond recognition, clearly symbolic of the unrest in the US over both civil-rights issues and the Vietnam War. It became an instant classic and the cry of the new generation. Hendrix died the following year in England in a barbiturate-induced coma.

⬟ *see* Kurt Cobain p. 87

▶ *RIGHT: Breakfast at Tiffany's star Audrey Hepburn.*

HEPBURN, AUDREY
(1929–93)

At the height of her career Belgian-born actress Audrey Hepburn appeared in the enduring films *Breakfast at Tiffany's* (1961), *Funny Face* (1957) and *Roman Holiday* (1953), all of which won her much acclaim and she earned a reputation as one of Hollywood's favourite darlings. She also won film-goers' hearts as Eliza Doolittle in *My Fair Lady*. After she retired from making films, she turned her attention to charity work and campaigned exhaustively for the United Nations. Her death in 1993 was greatly mourned and her reputation endures as the most familiar icon of 1950s and 1960s sophistication and elegance.

◘ *see* Brigette Bardot p. 80

HEPBURN, KATHARINE (1907–2003)

The only actress to earn four Oscars throughout her career, Katharine Hepburn is perhaps best loved for her portrayal of feisty, intelligent women in films such as *Bringing up Baby* (1937) and *Adam's Rib* (1949). She also starred with Humphrey Bogart in *The African Queen*.

➡ *see* Cary Grant p. 101, Spencer Tracey p. 130

HITCHCOCK, SIR ALFRED (1899–1980)

Bristish-born US film director and the undisputed master of the thriller genre in mid-twentieth-century cinema, Alfred Hitchcock's catalogue shows enormous narrative skill, from the classic *The Thirty-Nine Steps* (1935) to the immense impact of 1960's *Psycho*. He brought out magnificent performances from some of the greatest actors of the day.

➡ *see* Cary Grant p. 101

HOFFMAN, DUSTIN (b. 1937)

American actor Dustin Hoffman shot to fame in the seminal film *The Graduate* (1967). He received the Best Actor Oscar for *Kramer vs Kramer* in 1979 and again for *Rain Man* (1988). His roles have been diverse and he has proven himself to be an extremely versatile actor.

➡ *see* Tom Cruise p. 89

HOLLY, BUDDY (1936–59)

Buddy Holly, born Charles Hardin Holley, is considered one of the founding fathers of rock 'n' roll and one of its most influential artistes. He was born in Lubbock, Texas to a musical family and, as a teenager, was already singing professionally as part of a country duo. Holly formed his own band, The Crickets, and after the release of several highly successful songs, he and the Crickets toured the UK in March

1958. In the audience was a teenager named Paul McCartney, who later cited Holly as a primary influence (his band's name, The Beatles, was later chosen partly in homage to Holly's Crickets). In 1959, Holly split from The Crickets and began a solo tour with other notable performers including Ritchie Valens and J. P. Richardson (The Big Bopper). In February of that year, Holly, Valens and Richardson boarded a small jet that flew into a snow storm and crashed, killing the pilot and all but Holly's wife (she miscarried soon after). This event inspired singer Don McLean's popular 1971 ballad 'American Pie', and immortalized 3 February as 'The Day the Music Died'.

◆ *see* The Beatles p. 81

JACKSON, MICHAEL (b. 1958)

Born in Gary, Indiana, USA, the seventh of nine children, Jackson began performing at the age of five as the lead singer of the Jackson 5 – a group composed of Michael and four of his older brothers. In 1969 the Jackson 5 were discovered and signed to Motown Records and soon became national stars. With Motown Records, the Jackson 5 made 14 albums and Michael recorded four albums as a solo artist. In his career Michael Jackson has received a slew of awards including 18 Grammies. Estimates for his album sales worldwide range from 200 million to well over 300 million. His video *Thriller* is considered by some to be the best music video of all time. In what was perhaps the 'Golden Age' of the video clip, some of Jackson's videos were virtually short films with considerable plots, impressive special effects, and featuring Jackson's distinctive dance style. MTV and *Rolling Stone* recently named four of his songs among the 100 greatest pop songs of all time. Accusastions of child abuse have haunted him periodically throughout his career and appeared again in 2004.

◆ *see* Madonna p. 109

JOHN, ELTON (b. 1947)

Elton John was born Reginald Kenneth Dwight but changed his name by deed poll to Elton Hercules John. Working in a band called Bluesology throughout the mid to late 1960s, his first international hits came in 1971, including 'Your Song'. The lyrics, then and since, were written by chief collaborator Bernie Taupin. He went on to be one of the most successful recording artists in the 1970s. He continued to chart throughout the 1980s, all his hits featuring his distinctive piano playing. In 1997, he updated the lyrics of 'Candle In The Wind' (a song originally written about Marilyn Monroe) for a special version mourning the death of Diana, Princess of Wales. He continues to release new material to commercial success and tours extensively.

◆ see Diana, Princess of Wales p. 240

KEATON, BUSTER (1895–1966)

Buster Keaton's trademark was physical comedy with a deadpan expression; he was known as 'The Great Stone Face'. He was born into vaudeville. His godfather was the famous escapologist Harry Houdini, who dubbed him 'Buster' after seeing him, just six months old, tumble down a flight of stairs without injury. After stage came screen and Keaton began starring in a series of two-reel comedies before graduating to full-length features in the early 1920s. Keaton became one of the most famous comedians in the world. His popularity was eclipsed only by the giant success of Charlie Chaplin. Keaton and Chaplin shared the screen for only ten minutes in their lives, playing two ageing former vaudeville stars trying to recapture a bit of glory in Chaplin's late film *Limelight* (1952). In it Keaton remarks, 'If one more person tells me this is just like old times I swear I'll jump out the window'.

◆ see Charlie Chaplin p. 85

KUBRICK, STANLEY (1928–99)

Stanley Kubrick was an American film director born in New York. His films are highly acclaimed for their technical perfection and deep, intellectual symbolism. Kubrick was drawn to controversy in his choice of stories, as seen in his decision to film *Lolita* in 1960, in which the central character is sexually obsessed with pubescent girls. It was with *Lolita* that he discovered the talent of Peter Sellers. Kubrick asked Sellers to play four roles simultaneously in his next film, *Dr. Strangelove or: How I Learned to Stop Worrying and Love the Bomb* (1963). *Dr. Strangelove* is considered by many to be one of the greatest motion pictures of all time. His next two films, *2001: A Space Odyssey* (1968) and *A Clockwork Orange* (1971), are equally considered to be masterpieces of science-fiction cinema. Kubrick spent years of his life planning a film entitled *A.I.* (later made by Steven Spielberg in 2001), but he abandoned the project and chose to film *Eyes Wide Shut* (1999) instead. He completed the filming only days before his death.

◘ *see* Steven Spielberg p. 128

LAUREL, STAN (1890–1965) AND OLIVER HARDY (1892–1957)

Comic film actors Stan Laurel and Oliver Hardy first began working together in the 1926 short film *Slipping Wives*. They made over 20 feature-length films together and were much-loved in the early film era. Their comic antics have endured and the pair are still popular today.

◘ *see* Charlie Chaplin p. 85

LEE, BRUCE (1895–1966)

Bruce Lee is widely considered to be the greatest martial arts actor of the twentieth century, his own fighting style being based on Kung Fu. Lee was born Lee Jun-fan in San Francisco, USA, but raised in Hong

Kong. In 1959 he returned to the US to further his studies, majoring in philosophy at the University of Washington. He found his break as the star Kato in the television series *The Green Hornet*. After returning to Hong Kong, he starred in the movies that would cement his fame. His films, especially his last one, *Enter the Dragon* (1973), elevated the traditional martial-arts film to a new level, inspiring artists such as Jackie Chan and Chuck Norris. Bruce Lee died of cerebral oedema in 1973, the official cause of death being an allergic reaction to an analgesic he took. His son, Brandon Lee, was also a martial artist and an actor.

◆ *see* Jackie Chan p. 85

LEIGH, VIVIEN (1913–67)

The English actress Vivien Leigh came to fame when she won the part of Scarlett O'Hara in *Gone With the Wind* (1939). She won her first Oscar as a southern belle for this; her second came in 1951, for *A Streetcar Named Desire*. She was married to the great Shakespearean actor Sir Laurence Olivier.

◆ *see* Sir Laurence Olivier p. 119

LENNON, JOHN (1940–80)

English singer/songwriter and former member of The Beatles, Lennon's solo career included work with his wife Yoko Ono, producing definitive albums such as *John Lennon and the Plastic Ono Band* (1970) and *Imagine* (1971). During the late 1960s to early 1970s Lennon's work was often radical and extremely personal in content. Lennon was shot dead in New York in 1980 by an obsessive fan.

◆ *see* The Beatles p. 81, Paul McCartney p. 112

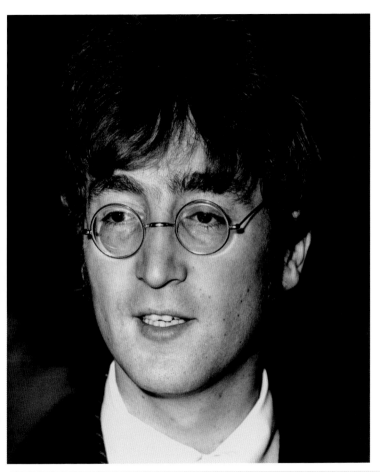

▲ ABOVE: The legendary John Lennon.

LLOYD WEBBER, SIR ANDREW (b. 1948)

Lloyd Webber met the lyricist Tim Rice in 1965 and within three years they had written *Joseph and His Amazing Technicolour Dreamcoat* (1968), which displays a strong lyricism amd a close affinity to pop. His most successful musical was *Cats*, based on the poems of T. S. Eliot, which was one of the longest-running shows in London and on Broadway. Lloyd Webber's musicals are essentially episodic, although he has shown an inclination to through-composition. He has also shown a desire to tackle more serious topics, in *The Beautiful Game* (2000), which explores issues surrounding Northern Ireland in the 1960s and 70s through the medium of a local football team.

◘ *see* T. S. Eliot p. 25

MADONNA (LOUISE CICCONE) (b. 1958)

US singer/songwriter and actress Madonna first burst on to the music scene in 1984. Since then she has proved herself a master of reinvention, conastantly changing her look and the style of her music. It is this that has ensured her longevity and she and is still producing best-selling, critically acclaimed music, such as her album *Music* (2000).

◘ *see* The Rolling Stones p. 123

MARLEY, BOB (1945–81)

Jamaican singer Bob Marley was born near Kingston, Jamaica. In his short life Marley became – and continues to be – the most commercially successful reggae artist of all time. He wrote, recorded and produced most of his music, whilst working with his band the Wailers.

◘ *see* The Rolling Stones p. 123

▶ *RIGHT: Bob Marley and the Wailers brought reggae to a worldwide audience.*

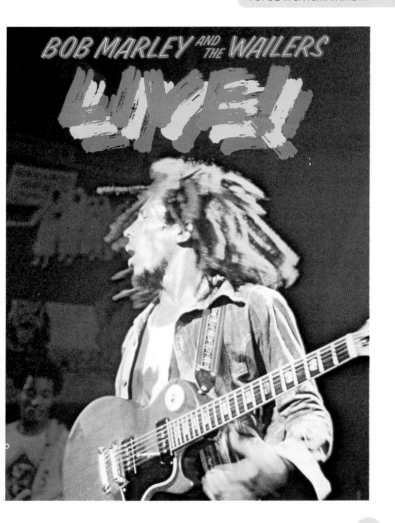

MASTROIANNI, MARCELLO (b. 1923)

Italian actor Marcello Mastroianni was made famous by the seminal film by Fellini *La Dolce Vita* (1959). He again worked for Fellini in *8½* (1963) and alongside Sophia Loren in *Marriage, Italian Style* (1963).

◆ *see* Isabella Rossellini p. 123

MCCARTNEY, PAUL (b. 1942)

Singer/songwriter and bass guitarist of The Beatles, McCartney released his eponymous solo album just weeks before the final Beatles album was released in 1970. He later formed his band Wings, with whom he enjoyed some success, particularly with the 1973 album *Band on the Run*. McCartney married the photographer Linda McCartney in 1969.

◆ *see* The Beatles p. 81 John Lennon p. 108

MCQUEEN, STEVE (1930–80)

Born Terence Steven McQueen in Beech Grove, Indiana, USA, Steve McQueen came to acting via the Marines. In 1952, he took advantage of the 'GI Bill' to study at the Actors' Studio in New York, making his Broadway debut in 1955 in *A Hatful of Rain*. McQueen moved into film in 1956 with *Somebody Up There Likes Me*. His real breakthrough came in 1963 with *The Great Escape*, and his fame peaked in 1968 with *Bullitt*. To work on this film with its memorable car-chase was for him a dream. McQueen was a motorcycle and race-car enthusiast and, when he had the opportunity, he would do his own driving, not allowing a stuntman to do it for him. After *The Towering Inferno* in 1974, McQueen did not return to film until 1978, when he played in *An Enemy of the People*. After 1978 he appeared only in two further films before his death in November 1980.

◆ *see* Paul Newman p. 118

Paul McCartney has enjoyed continued success as a solo musician.

MERCURY, FREDDIE (1946–91)

Freddie Mercury was born Faroukh Bulsara in Zanzibar and was the lead singer with Queen, a British rock band of the 1970s, 80s and 90s. With a wide vocal range and a somewhat operatic technique, he was one of the most technically accomplished singers to work in the pop idiom, as well as the composer of many of Queen's hits, including 'Bohemian Rhapsody', 'Somebody to Love' and 'We Are the Chanpions'. He also had hits as a solo artist, but did not gain his first solo number one until after his death, with 'Living On My Own'. He died of AIDS on 24 November 1991, in London.

🔸 see The Rolling Stones p. 123

MILLIGAN, SPIKE (1918–2002)

Spike Milligan, comedian, novelist, poet and jazz musician, was born Terence Alan Milligan in Ahmed Nagar, India, to an Irish-born officer in the British army. Though he lived most of his life in Britain and served in the army, he was declared stateless in 1960, and took Irish citizenship. Milligan made his reputation in the 1950s in *The Goon Show* on radio. He originated the idea, wrote much of the zany fantasy in the programme and played many of the parts. He was the master of the surreal and his humour was often anarchic and frequently unexpected. Milligan was a towering influence on British comedy, taking music hall ideas and weaving into them his own hilarious absurdities.

🔸 see Peter Sellers p. 126

MITCHELL, JONI (b. 1943)

Born Roberta Joan Anderson in Fort McLeod, Alberta, Canada, Joni Mitchell was first associated with the folk music scene of the mid-1960s in New York City. Through the 1970s she expanded her horizons, predominantly to rock music and jazz, to become one of the most highly respected singer-songwriters of the late twentieth century. Mitchell was inducted into the Canadian Music Hall of Fame in 1981 and into the Rock and Roll Hall of Fame in 1997. She received a Grammy Award for Lifetime Achievement in 2002, with a citation describing her as 'one of the most important female recording artists of the rock era'.

◆ *see* Bob Dylan p. 95

MONROE, MARILYN (1926–62)

Born in Los Angeles, Norma Jean Mortenson became a photographic model at the age of 20, after which a series of small movie parts led quickly to stardom in films like *Gentlemen Prefer Blondes* (1953) and *Some Like it Hot* (1959). Though increasingly uncomfortable with her type-casting as giggly dumb blonde, she struggled to make an impact in more serious roles, while her marriages to baseball star Joe di Maggio and playwright Arthur Miller both ended unhappily. Her suicide saw her stereotyped again, this time as iconic victim of Hollywood's destructive hunger for youth and beauty, and this is how her image has come down to later generations. (*See over for illustration.*)

◆ *see* Elvis Presley p. 120

MOORE, ROGER (b. 1927)

Sir Roger Moore is an English actor who first made his name with appearances in the TV series *Maverick*, *The Saint* (as Simon Templar) and *The Persuaders*. Then in 1972 his name became immortalized when he was asked to become James Bond. He appeared in seven Bond movies: *Live and Let Die* (1973), *The Man with the Golden Gun* (1974), *The Spy*

▼ *OVER: 1950s Hollywood icon Marilyn Monroe.*

Who Loved Me (1977), *Moonraker* (1979), *For Your Eyes Only* (1981), *Octopussy* (1983) and *A View to a Kill* (1985). Moore is now engaged in humanitarian projects in his work as an UNICEF ambassador. In the summer of 2003, Moore was made an Officer in the Most Excellent Order of the British Empire.

◆ *see* Sean Connery p. 87

MOREAU, JEANNE (b. 1928)

French actress Jeanne Moreau was acclaimed for her parts in New Wave films and is best remembered for her role the classic *Jules et Jim* (1962), Moreau also directed with *Lumière* (1975).

◆ *see* Brigitte Bardot p. 80

NEWMAN, PAUL (b. 1925)

Paul Newman is an American actor and film director and was one of Hollywood's leading male stars of the 1960s and 1970s. He fought in the Pacific Theater during World War II and returned to America, where he became a successful stage actor on Broadway. His first movie, *The Silver Chalice* (1954), has been described by Newman as the 'worst movie of the entire 50s decade' but he rebounded with a series of acclaimed roles. Amongst them were *Butch Cassidy and the Sundance Kid* (1969) and *The Sting* (1973). After many nominations, he finally received the Academy Award for Best Actor for his role in *The Color of Money* (1986).

◆ *see* Robert Redford p. 122

NICHOLSON, JACK (b. 1937)

US stage and screen actor Jack Nicholson plays the villain superbly; from zany (*Batman* 1989) to psychotic (*The Shining* 1980), Nicholson has been applauded for his unique style. One of Hollywood's brat-pack of the Marlon Brando era, Nicholson also won acclaim for his anti-hero McMurphy in *One Flew Over the Cuckoo's Nest* (1975). In later years he has turned his hand to comedy, in which he has seen equal success.

🔾 *see* Marlon Brando p. 83

OLIVIER, LORD LAURENCE (1907–89)

Arguably the greatest English stage actor in history, Laurence Olivier also made many films. His greatest achievements were in performances of Shakespeare, a genre he made entirely his own. Amongst the best-known of these are *Hamlet* (1948) and *Henry V* (1945), which Olivier also directed. He was married for some time to the English actress-turned-Hollywood-starlet Vivien Leigh.

🔾 *see* Vivien Leigh p. 108

PACINO, AL (b. 1940)

Al Pacino established himself during one of film's greatest decades, the 1970s, and has become an enduring and iconic figure in the world of American movies. He began his acting career on the stage, earning an Obie and a Tony Award along the way, but it was with the part of Michael Corleone in *The Godfather* (1972) that he made his mark on screen. Director Francis Ford Coppola had his heart set on the unknown Italian Pacino. The role was a career-making hit, and earned him his first Academy Award nomination for Best Supporting Actor. Another vicious gangster role cemented his legendary status in the ultra-violent *Scarface* (1973). After numerous nominations, he finally won the Academy Award for Best Actor for his amazing performance in *Scent of a Woman* (1992).

🔾 *see* Francis Ford Coppola p. 88

PALIN, MICHAEL (b. 1943)

Michael Palin was born in Sheffield, Yorkshire, England. He is famous for being a member of *Monty Python's Flying Circus*, in which he generally played roles that called for manic enthusiasm (such as the lumberjack of 'The Lumberjack Song') or unflappable calmness (such as the 'Dead Parrot' vendor). As the latter, he was often the perfect foil to the rising ire of characters portrayed by John Cleese. After *Monty Python*, Palin collaborated with fellow Python Terry Jones on the television comedy series *Ripping Yarns* (1977–79). In later years, Palin rejoined Cleese for the movies *A Fish Called Wanda* (1988) and *Fierce Creatures* (1997). More recently, he is known as the presenter of several series of travel programmes.

◆ *see* John Cleese p. 85

PRESLEY, ELVIS (1935–77)

Born in Tupelo, Mississippi, Elvis Aron Presley first sang as a boy in his Pentecostalist Church choir. A record privately made for his mother marked his breakthrough when it was heard by a Memphis music producer. Consciously on the look-out for a white singer who could sing black rhythm and blues, Sun Records' Sam Phillips instantly recognized the raw energy of Presley's talent. The great rock-and-roll success of the 1950s was followed by what many came to see as a long decline, as, under the management of 'Colonel' Tom Parker, Elvis made middle-of-the-road records and starred in mediocre films. His career gained momentum again in the 1970s, when an almost self-parodying version of the star appeared in Las Vegas to delight an audience that had aged along with him. Overweight and groggy with drugs, he died in 1977 at his Memphis home: the house, Graceland, is now a shrine for his still-adoring public.

◆ *see* The Beatles p. 81

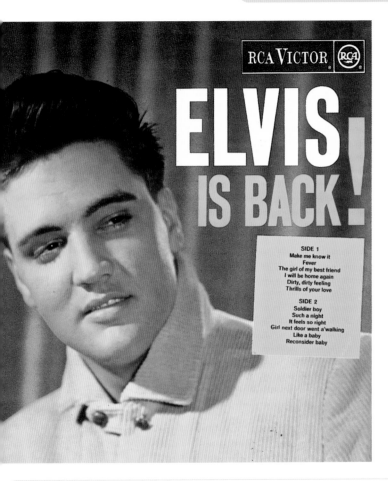

RCA VICTOR

ELVIS IS BACK!

SIDE 1
Make me know it
Fever
The girl of my best friend
I will be home again
Dirty, dirty feeling
Thrills of your love

SIDE 2
Soldier boy
Such a night
It feels so right
Girl next door went a'walking
Like a baby
Reconsider baby

▲ *ABOVE: Elvis Presley, the first rock 'n' roll star.*

REDFORD, ROBERT (b. 1937)

Robert Redford at first pursued a career as an artist, studying at the Pratt Institute of Art and living a painter's life in Europe. He subsequently studied acting in New York at the American Academy of Dramatic Arts. TV and stage experience coupled with all-American good looks led to movies and a breakthrough role in *Butch Cassidy and the Sundance Kid* (1969), followed by a string of box-office hits. In 1980 he started the Sundance Institute for aspiring, independent filmmakers. Its annual film festival has become one of the world's most influential. Redford's directorial debut, *Ordinary People* (1981), won him the Academy Award for Best Director. He gained further critical acclaim with *A River Runs Though It* (1992) and again with *Quiz Show* (1994), which earned him another Best Director nomination.

◆ *see* Paul Newman p. 118

REDGRAVE, SIR MICHAEL (1908–85)

British actor Michael Redgrave starred in films such as *The Lady Vanishes* (1938) but his main love was for the theatre. He was the father of Corin, Vanessa and Lynn Redgrave, all of whom have had successsful acting careers.

◆ *see* Sir Aledc Guinness p. 102

ROBERTS, JULIA (b. 1967)

American film actress Julia Roberts shot to fame playing the 'hooker with a heart' in the box office smash *Pretty Woman* (1990), alongside Richard Gere. She hasn't looked back since this time and now has a series of hits under her belt, a string of broken engagements to some of the film industry's hottest male stars, and is one of the highest-paid actresses in Hollywood. She won the best actress Oscar for *Erin Brockovich* (2000).

◆ *see* Tom Cruise p. 89

ROGERS, GINGER (1911–95)

The American actress and dancer Ginger Rogers is most famously associated with Fred Astaire, with whom she made several well-known films in which the couple's dance routines were much-lauded. After the duo split, Rogers found some continued success with her film career, most notably for her Oscar-winning role in *Kitty Foyle* (1940).

◆ see Fred Astaire p. 80

ROLLING STONES, THE (1962)

The Rolling Stones were formed in London in 1962, and at the time their hard-rock anthems and general bad behaviour were marketed as the opposition to The Beatles' wholesome tunes and good-guy image. Remarkably, despite several band member changes (and deaths), the Stones are still recording and playing music together. Mick Jagger and Keith Richards are the key writers of their predominantly rhythm-and-blues orientated rock music. (*See over for illustration.*)

◆ see The Beatles p. 81

ROSSELLINI, ISABELLA (b. 1952)

One of twin daughters born to actress Ingrid Bergman and director Roberto Rossellini, Isabella Rossellini did not plan to pursue the family business. She worked as a translator and television journalist, but in 1976 was persuaded to take a small part in her mother's film *A Matter of Time*. She found acting to her liking, and was cast in her first big-screen starring role in *The Meadow* (1979). In the early 1980s, Rossellini put her film activities on hold to concentrate on her modelling career. After her first marriage to Hollywood director Martin Scorsese ended in 1983, she began a relationship with ballet star Mikhail Baryshnikov, with whom she co-starred in *White Nights* (1985). She was later

involved with filmmaker David Lynch, who cast her in her break-through role as a much-abused small-town nightclub singer in *Blue Velvet* (1986).

▶ *see* Martin Scorsese p. 125

SCORSESE, MARTIN (b. 1942)

Martin Scorsese has been called the 'greatest living American director', and several of his movies occupy spots on the American Film Institute's list of 'greatest movies'. He was associated with the 'movie brats' of the 1970s: Francis Ford Coppola, Steven Spielberg, George Lucas and Brian De Palma. It was De Palma who introduced him to Robert De Niro, with whom he has worked in many projects.

Scorsese's first movie starring De Niro was *Mean Streets* (1973). Again casting De Niro, Scorsese made his first lasting mark on the world of the movies with *Taxi Driver* (1976), for which he received Oscar nominations for Best Picture and Best Director. He cast De Niro again in *Raging Bull* (1980), which came to be viewed as a masterpiece. Whilst his low-budget making of *The Last Temptation of Christ* (1988) caused a public furore, it was not until *Goodfellas* (1990) that he again caught the eye of critics and movie-goers. This story of life as a gangster has been called the greatest 'Mob movie' since *The Godfather*, and it secured Scorsese a place among the all-time greatest motion-picture directors.

▶ *see* Robert De Niro p. 89

◀ LEFT: *One of the most enduring bands of all time, The Rolling Stones were a 1960s and 70s phenomenon.*

▶ *RIGHT: Star of the* Pink Panther *films, Peter Sellers.*

SELLERS, PETER (1925–80)

English comedian Peter Sellers began his career in radio as a member of extremely successful comic group *The Goon Show*. On film, he is best remembered as the inept police investigator Inspector Clouseau in the numerous *Pink Panther* films.

◆ *see* Spike Milligan p. 114

SIMPSON, BART (b. 1989)

Bart Simpson is the son of Homer Jay and Marge Bouvier Simpson and brother to Lisa and baby Maggie. The reassuringly dysfunctional family star in the TV show *The Simpsons*, the creation of Matt Groening. Bart is a misunderstood and often wayward child, but he has a lot of decent qualities: he looks out for his sister, Lisa, and he has befriended outcasts and misfits like Milhouse Van Houten and Ralph Wiggum. That said, he is not a typical ten-year-old: he has starred in his own short-lived TV series (with his idol, Krusty the Clown), spotted and named a comet that nearly destroyed his home-town of Springfield, singlehandedly brought a homicidal TV sidekick to justice – twice – and almost got the role of Fallout Boy in the *Radioactive Man* movie.

◆ *see* Walt Disney p. 95

SINATRA, FRANK (1915–98)

Frank Sinatra is one of the top musicians of the twentieth century and arguably the most famous member of the Rat Pack, of which the other members were Dean Martin and Sammy Davis Jr. Sinatra decided to become a singer after hearing Bing Crosby on the radio. He began singing in small clubs in New Jersey and eventually attracted the attention of

trumpeter and band-leader Harry James. His rapid rise to fame revealed a whole new audience for popular music, which had generally appealed to adults up to that time. He was the first teen idol. His voice is instantly recognizable, and evokes not only great strength and charisma, but also nostalgia and tenderness. He also had a career as a film actor, his most notable appearances being in *From Here to Eternity* (1953), *The Man with the Golden Arm* (1955) and *The Manchurian Candidate* (1962).

◆ *see* Glenn Miller p. 45

SPIELBERG, STEVEN (b. 1947)

Phenomenally successful film director Steven Spielberg's career took off following the hit *Jaws* (1975). A string of hits followed and he soon became the most sought-after director in Hollywood. Although he is best-known for audience-pleasing family blockbusters, in later years Spielberg has proven his expertise in other genres and most particularly earned admiration for his more serious films such *Schindler's List* (1993). Most recently he has embarked on an equally successful joint project with the actor Tom Hanks in the television serial *Band of Brothers* – a no-holds-barred account of the experiences of an American army company during World War II.

◆ *see* Oscar Schindler p. 282

STEWART, JAMES (1908–97)

US actor James Stewart is best-remembered for his starring role in the 1946 quintessential Christmas film, *It's a Wonderful Life*. However, it was for *The Philadelphia Story* (1940) that Stewart won his Oscar. He was one of the many actors of his generation to be tempted by Hitchcock's horror genre, and was much praised for his part in Hitchcock's *Vertigo* (1958).

◆ *see* Alfred Hitchcock p. 104

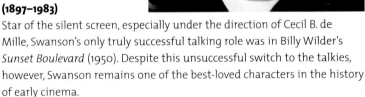

▶ *RIGHT: American film actress Meryl Streep.*

STREEP, MERYL (b. 1949)

The distinguished American actress Meryl Streep's first major film role was in *The Deer Hunter* (1978) and her career sky-rocketed from this point onwards. She has won Oscars for *Kramer vs Kramer* (1979) and for *Sophie's Choice* (1982).

◆ *see* Jack Nicholson p. 118

SWANSON, GLORIA (1897–1983)

Star of the silent screen, especially under the direction of Cecil B. de Mille, Swanson's only truly successful talking role was in Billy Wilder's *Sunset Boulevard* (1950). Despite this unsuccessful switch to the talkies, however, Swanson remains one of the best-loved characters in the history of early cinema.

◆ *see* Charlie Chaplin. 85

TARANTINO, QUENTIN (b. 1963)

Quentin Tarantino rapidly rose to fame in the early 1990s as a fresh and gritty storyteller who brought new life to even the most stereotypical of American archetypes. His big break came with his screenplay for *True Romance* (1993), which was directed by Tony Scott and starred Rosanna

Arquette and Christian Slater. He was launched to stardom with his directorial debut, *Reservoir Dogs* (1993), in which he also acted in a limited role. A stylish but bloody movie, this set the tone for his later films. The follow up, *Pulp Fiction* (1994), was a complex film with a similarly brutal wit and many excellent performances. It was noted for reviving the career of John Travolta. His most recent film is a highly stylized revenge flick told in two parts: *Kill Bill Vol. I* (2003) and *Kill Bill Vol. II* (2004).

◄ *see* Steven Spielberg. 128

TAYLOR, ELIZABETH (b. 1932)
English-born actress Elizabeth Taylor is as famous for her many marriages as she is for her acting. As a child star, Taylor received her highest praise during the 1950s and 60s for films such as *A Place in the Sun* (1951) and *Butterfield 8* (1960). She famously married Richard Burton.

◄ *see* Richard Burton p. 84

TRACEY, SPENCER (1900–67)
American actor Spencer Tracey was romantically linked with co-star Katharine Hepburn. He exemplified American ideals with his unpretentious sincerity in films such as *Woman of the Year* (1942) and *Inherit the Wind* (1960).

◄ *see* Katharine Hepburn p. 104

WAYNE, JOHN (1907–79)
The career of John Wayne, also known as the Duke, spanned the evolutionary phase of American cinema, appearing in both silent movies and 'talkies'. He was born Marion Morrison in Winterset, Iowa, USA, and his family moved to Glendale, California in 1911. There, neighbours started calling him Big Duke, because he never went anywhere without his

Airedale dog, Little Duke. The name stuck for the rest of his life. His first starring role was in the movie *The Big Trail* (1930); it was the director of that movie, Raoul Walsh, who gave him his stage name, after Revolutionary War general 'Mad Anthony' Wayne. Wayne played the male lead in 142 of his film appearances, mostly westerns and war films, an as yet unsurpassed record. Despite his prolific output, Wayne won only a single Best Leading Actor Oscar, for *True Grit* (1969).

see Clint Eastwood p. 97

WEST, MAE (1892–1980)

Although she starred in less than a dozen films, American actress Mae West still left an indelible impression on the movie world. Her roles (reflections of her caricatured self), were all overtly sexual, sharp-witted women and she became an icon of her time.

see Katharine Hepburn p. 104

WINFREY, OPRAH (b. 1954)

Oprah Winfrey, born in Kosciusko, Mississippi, USA, is one of the most successful entrepreneurs in America. She started as a Baltimore news anchor. Soon she had her own daytime talk show, *The Oprah Winfrey Show* (later abbreviated to *Oprah*). Winfrey began to do huge amounts of work for charity and feature people in need on her show. By the late 1990s she had a powerful media influence. She publishes her own magazine, called *O*, and has her own cable television network, called Oxygen. Winfrey has also ventured into acting, most notably in the screen adaptation of the Alice Walker novel *The Color Purple* (1982), for which she received an Oscar nomination. Winfrey is also a published author, and in 2002 she received a special Emmy award called The Bob Hope Humanitarian Award.

see Audrey Hepburn p. 103

SPORT

AGASSI, ANDRÉ (b. 1970)

Only two years after turning professional, the American André Agassi, won six tennis tournaments in a single season (1988). Agassi was remarkable for the great accuracy and power he produced with a minimum of physical effort. In all, he won eight Grand Slam tournaments, 49 other singles titles, one doubles title and the Olympic gold medal in 1996. In 1997, however, he suffered such a critical loss of form that he sank to 141st in the world rankings. Determined to rebuild his career, Agassi played in the second-string Challenger tournaments to improve his ranking. By the end of 1999, he was ranked number one, and in that year won the French Open: this completed his 'career' Grand Slam, the winning of all four Slams over the years, a feat achieved by only four other male players. Agassi married the women's champion tennis player Steffi Graf in 2001.

⬥ see Steffi Graf p. 171

ALI, MOHAMMED (b. 1942)

Mohammed Ali was the first man to win three heavyweight-boxing titles.

Born Cassius Marcellus Clay in Louisville, USA, he started boxing in 1954, winning amateur championships including the Olympic Games. He defeated Sonny Liston (February 1964), Ernie Terrell (February 1967), lost to Joe Frazier (March 1971), defeated Frazier (January 1974), defeated George Foreman (October 1974), lost to Leon Spinks (February 1978) and defeated Spinks (September 1978). Ali remains the best-known boxer of all time and still receives awards for his achievements.

see George Foreman p. 168

BAGGIO, ROBERTO (b. 1967)

One of Italy's most fêted-strikers of the last 20 years, the more talented Baggio brother played all his club football during the golden years of Serie A. A move outside Italy was never considered, not least because no one outside Serie A could afford the transfer fee. An outstanding schoolboy talent, he made his 1983 debut for Vicenza aged 15 and was snapped up by Fiorentina after only two years. His £8 million transfer in 1990 to Juventus sparked street riots, but it was five years before his goals finally won Serie A for the Turin giants.

A star of the Azzuri, his goals saw Italy through to the final of the 1994 World Cup, but the match proved to be his nadir. The memory of Baggio's final penalty sailing harmlessly over the bar to hand Brazil the trophy probably haunts him still, and started a decline that saw his previously unthinkable omission from the Euro 96 squad. A contentious choice for France 98, his chance to lay the World Cup ghost was unsuccessful as Italy again lost on penalties to the eventual winners. (*See over for illustration.*)

see David Beckham p. 145

◀ *LEFT: Three-times heavyweight boxing champion Mohammed Ali.*

▲ ABOVE: *Baggio despairs after missing the final penalty in the 1994 World Cup Final.*

BANKS, GORDON (b. 1937)

England's post-war tradition is richer in goalkeepers than in any other position. The pick of a distinguished crop is a man once sacked from Romarsh Welfare in the Yorkshire League after conceding 15 goals in two games. Fortunately for England, Gordon Banks put this disappointment behind him to become his country's automatic choice for nine years, making his debut in Alf Ramsey's second game in charge. It was Ramsey who gave him all his 73 caps, but his worth to England's cause was perhaps most tellingly illustrated by a game he missed. Stricken by a stomach bug the night before the 1970 World Cup quarter-final against

West Germany in Mexico, Banks was forced to watch helplessly as his replacement, Peter Bonetti, conceded three goals as England let slip a 2-0 lead. Despite his ability, Banks's club career was largely unsuccessful. The end of his career made headline news for the wrong reasons, the loss of the sight in his right eye following a car crash making his fitness and athleticism irrelevant.

see Peter Shilton p. 213

▲ ABOVE: Star of 1970s goalkeeping, Gordon Banks.

BANNISTER, ROGER (b. 1929)

Running a mile in four minutes or less had been a quest for middle-distance athletes since 1861, when the record for the mile stood at 4 minutes 55 seconds. Over the next 93 years, seconds were shaved off this time until in 1945, it stood at 4.01.3 minutes. Then, on 6 May 1954, Roger Bannister, a medical student and experienced amateur athlete, ran the distance at Iffley Road, Oxford. He broke the four-minute barrier by less than two seconds to register a new record of 3.59.4 minutes. The effort had been tremendous. Bannister ended the race in a state of near-collapse, gasping for breath. It was not long before two or even three front-runners in races were breaking the four-minute mile in their turn, and coming out of it in much better shape than the heroic Roger Bannister.

◆ see Sebastian Coe p. 159

◀ LEFT: Roger Bannister breaking the four-minute mile.

BATISTUTA, GABRIEL OMAR (b. 1969)

As a teenager Gabriel Omar Batistuta seemed destined to be a basketball star, but a switch to football at the age of 17 saw a remarkable turn-around. Not the quickest, but hard-working, powerful and sharp, the striker with the rock-star looks made an instant impact. 'Batigol' won the Copa Libertadores (Argentinean championship) at 19, and was top scorer as Argentina won the Copa América for the first time in 32 years in 1991. The inevitable move to Italy followed, but to Fiorentina, the Viola, not one of the Serie A giants. Despite his goals Fiorentina were relegated, but Batigol stayed, and they came back up. In 1999 the Viola pushed hard for the title, but a crucial injury to Batistuta cost them dearly. Finally, in 2000, he left for Roma, and promptly inspired them to a Serie A title triumph, a victory his ability and commitment fully merited.

Batistuta played with distinction in two World Cup tournaments in his time at Fiorentina, proving he lacked no appetite for the big games. The 2002 finals proved to be Batistuta's swansong, as age and creaky legs caught up with him.

see Diego Maradona p. 190

BECKENBAUER, FRANZ (b. 1945)

'The Kaiser', as Franz Beckenbauer became known (such were the imperious nature of his displays for club and country), was one of the finest players in the history of the game. An outstanding captain and tactician, it was no surprise that he went on to win everything, including the World Cup as player and manager.

Beginning his international career as a deep-lying midfielder, Beckenbauer revolutionized the notion of the attacking sweeper, bursting out of defence to set up attacks, often even finishing them himself. He had every attribute a footballer requires: control, passing, strength and uncanny vision. Only Ruud Gullit has since shown a comparable range of skills, but he lacked Beckenbauer's iron will. Retiring from international football in 1977, Beckenbauer teamed up with Pelé at New York Cosmos in the North American Soccer League, before returning to claim one last domestic honour with SV Hamburg.

Once retired he was appointed national coach almost immediately, and injected the same discipline and indomitable steel into the German side in the 1980s that it was famed for under his captaincy ten years earlier. More success followed, and Beckenbauer, as President of Bayern Munich, remains at the forefront of German and European football to this day. (*See over for illustration.*)

see Sven Goran Eriksson p. 162

◀ *LEFT: Argentinean star Gabriel Batistuta.*

▲ ABOVE: Beckenbauer holds the World Cup with the West German team in 1974.

BECKER, BORIS (b. 1967)

When he was only 17, Boris Becker achieved three records by winning the coveted Wimbledon tennis title: he was the first German, the first unseeded player and the youngest person to become Wimbledon champion. Becker's size, great power and imposing personality made him a formidable opponent and he dominated men's tennis with his huge serve and hard-driving volleys across the net. This, together with his great athleticism, made Becker the best player on grass during the 1980s. Becker won five Grand Slam titles – the Australian Open (1991), Wimbledon (1965, 1986, 1989) and the US Open (1989). He also claimed 44 other singles titles and 15 doubles.

see Pete Sampras p. 207

RIGHT: A young Boris Becker raises the trophy at Wimbledon.

◀ LEFT: David Beckham celebrates a goal.

BECKHAM, DAVID (b. 1975)

When David Beckham curled a last-minute free kick over the Greek wall to win England a place at the 2002 World Cup finals, it completed a comeback more remarkable than merely the context of England's qualifying campaign. It completed a transformation in the public's perception of the England captain. Three years previously Beckham had been a national figure of hate, reviled after his petulant kick and red card during the game against Argentina had contributed to England's defeat in the second round at France 98. His passing and crossing are of the highest order, and his shooting from set pieces is almost Brazilian in its power and accuracy.

That he has matured beyond adolescent cockiness is more surprising, not least because his looks, style and pop-star wife have made 'Becks' the most hounded footballer since George Best. Beckham continues to astound the world with his expertise on the pitch, but now he does it from Madrid, where he moved in 2003 to play for Real after arguments with United boss Alex Ferguson.

◆ see George Best p. 145

BEST, GEORGE (b. 1946)

'I think I've found you a genius,' claimed the Belfast scout in an excited telephone call to Matt Busby. He wasn't wrong. Signed as a professional on his seventeenth birthday, George Best thrilled the Old Trafford faithful like no player before or since. Had Best played for a stronger country than Northern Ireland he may now be spoken of with the same reverence as Pelé.

The cocktail of outrageous ball skills and smouldering good looks proved to be an explosive one; Best's transformation from Belfast innocent to international playboy seemed to capture the spirit of the 1960s. He was even dubbed 'El Beatle' by the Portuguese press after a mesmerizing display in Benfica's Stadium of Light. The free spirit that was Europe's most feared striker became society's hottest property, an advertiser's dream whose fame and fortune rocketed in a whirl of boutique openings and product endorsement. The inevitable falls from grace were frequent and glaring, and at 28 he was washed-up. Despite an Indian summer at Fulham with fellow funster Rodney Marsh, and occasional spells in the NASL and elsewhere, the career of George Best has now been restricted to bar-room reminiscences for nearly 30 years.

◐ *see* David Beckham p. 146

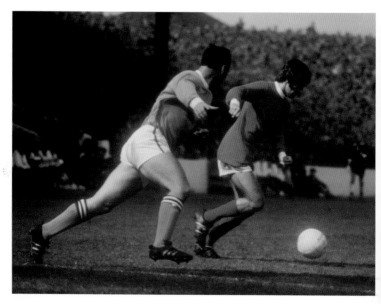

BORG, BJORN (b. 1956)

Bjorn Borg is a Swedish tennis player, who attained a total of 11 Grand Slam singles championships and 62 singles tournaments during his career. Borg was the number one ranked player during six different stretches between 1977 and 1981. Borg was noted for his baseline style of play and great endurance, and dubbed 'The Ice Man' for his calm court demeanor. Along with Jimmy Connors and John McEnroe, Borg elevated the game of tennis to new levels of popularity that were never seen before. Borg's most famous match was probably his five-set win in the 1980 Wimbledon final over McEnroe. He retired in 1983, at the age of 26 and, in 1987, was inducted into the International Tennis Hall of Fame in Newport, Rhode Island.

see John McEnroe p. 193

BOTHAM, IAN (b. 1955)

In the 1980s, one man bestrode English cricket like no other in the modern era: Ian Botham. From the very beginning of the decade, when he was England captain at just 24 years of age, to its end, Botham's influence on English cricket was unparalleled. His achievements with both bat and ball will never be forgotten. An immensely talented all-rounder, deeply committed to winning and a genuine crowd-pleaser, Botham was an incomparable hero. He will always be remembered for how he destroyed the Australians in the summer of 1981 with performances that went beyond superlatives and assured for him a legendary status in English sport. (*See over for illustration.*)

see Don Bradman p. 149

◄ *LEFT: George Best in his heyday.*

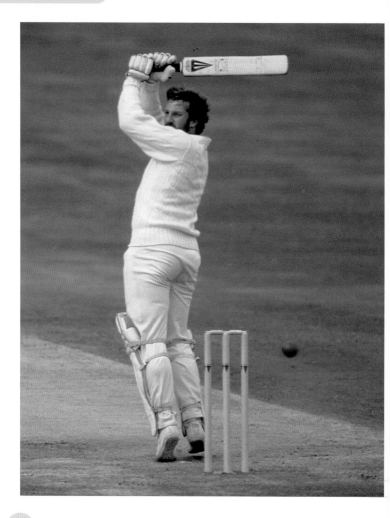

BRADMAN, DON
(1908–2001)

▲ *ABOVE: Don Bradman.*

Widely regarded as the greatest cricketer of all time, the career of champion batsman Donald Bradman lasted for 18 years, from 1930. He captained the Australian Test team (1936–48) and broke scoring records in first-class and international cricket matches. In 1930, he achieved a top score of 334 runs not out, which remains a record today. Bradman was considered so dangerous as a batsman that the 'bodyline' bowling technique was used in the Test series against England in 1932–33 to counteract his dominance. Bradman played in 52 Test matches, retiring with a batting average of 99.94 runs. Bradman was awarded a knighthood in 1949 and was made Companion of the Order of Australia, the country's highest civil award, in 1979.

◘ *see* Ian Botham p. 147

◄ *LEFT: Ian Botham.*

BUSBY, MATT (1909–94)

In 1945 Matt Busby became manager of Manchester United, a club whose 67 years had yielded just two league titles and a solitary FA Cup. The trophy cabinet had been bare for 34 years, Old Trafford was a bomb site and United were lodging at Maine Road. On his retirement in 1969, Busby had added five Championships, two FA Cups and United had become England's first winners of the European Cup.

Although a remarkable haul, it would surely have been more but for the tragic Munich air crash in 1958 that robbed English football of one of its greatest-ever teams. It was indicative of his tenacity and strength of will that Busby not only cheated death himself in the disaster but that, within seven years, he had made United champions again, rebuilding his team around George Best, Denis Law and Bobby Charlton. The end of his tenure saw them relegated within five years.

A journey to Old Trafford today finishes with a walk down Sir Matt Busby Way to his statue. One senses a modest, hard-working Scotsman from humble, working-class origins would have been uneasy with such acclaim. However, for a club with legends to spare, it is fitting that the tribute is for him alone.

◆ see George Best p. 145

CAMPBELL, DONALD (1921–67)

Donald Campbell was born in Horley, Surrey, England, the son of Sir Malcolm Campbell. Following his father's career he strove to set speed records on land and water, also in vehicles named *Bluebird*. Campbell set seven world water-speed records between 1955 and 1964. In 1964 he set the water-speed record of 649 kph at Lake Eyre Salt Flats, Australia. On 31 December 1964, at Dumbleyung Lake, also in Australia, he reached 444.6 kph. In doing so, he became the first person to set both water and

▼ BELOW: Football manager Sir Matt Busby.

land records in the same year. He died three years later, on 4 January 1967, when his *Bluebird* K7 flipped and disintegrated at around 450 kph on Coniston Water in England.

◆ see Malcolm Campbell p. 152

CAMPBELL, MALCOLM (1885–1948)

Malcolm Campbell gained the world speed record on land and on water at various times during the 1920s and 1930s using vehicles called *Bluebird*. His son, Donald Campbell, died attempting to repeat his achievements 30 years later. He also competed in Grand Prix motor racing, winning the 1927 and 1928 Grand Prix de Boulogne in France, driving a Bugatti T39A.

◆ *see* Donald Campbell p. 150

CANTONA, ERIC (b. 1966)

Whether for his footballing exploits or temperamental outbursts, few players have provoked headlines or incited debate like Eric Cantona.

An instant hit at Leeds, his arrival provided the Yorkshire club with the impetus to clinch the League title in 1992 but, while the fans idolized him, rumours of his clashes with manager Howard Wilkinson were rife. His shock £1.2 million transfer to Manchester United indicated Leeds' desire to be rid of him, but it turned out to be the most injudicious transfer sale of all time, as Cantona went on to inspire United to a period of domination unrivalled since Liverpool's run of success in the 1970s and 1980s.

It is a sad fact that Cantona will be remembered for one moment of madness when, at Crystal Palace in 1995, making his way off the pitch following yet another red card, Cantona launched a two-footed kung fu kick at a spectator who had racially abused him. A less gifted player may have been sacked, but Cantona survived and returned to lead United to more championship success. He retired at 31, and his recent incarnations as an actor and sports promoter have enhanced his reputation as the modern renaissance footballer.

◆ *see* Alan Shearer p. 213

▶ RIGHT: *Eric Cantona.*

CHARLTON, BOBBY (b. 1937)

Having survived the Munich air crash, Bobby Charlton seized his chance to become one of England's most successful and admired players. He never commanded the huge transfer fees paid for Denis Law, nor could he boast the natural flair and ability of George Best, but in terms of achievement Charlton was by far the most successful of United's most famous forward line. His application was total. As a young player he would often train wearing just a slipper on his right foot – a ploy designed to make him practise shooting with his left until it could generate the same venomous power as his right.

For England, he became a national hero after helping them win the 1966 World Cup, but it was his substitution in the 1970 quarter-final against Germany that fans remember almost as vividly; brought off by Alf Ramsey with the score at 2-1 to England, Charlton's absence upset the balance of the team and they eventually capitulated 3-2. Charlton bowed out in 1973 – on the same day as his brother, Jack – when over 60,000 fans packed Old Trafford for his testimonial. Knighted in 1994, he remains a director at Old Trafford and ambassador for both United and the Football Association.

◆ see Jack Charlton p. 155

CHARLTON, JACK (b. 1935)

An England World-Cup winner he may have been, and the defensive rock of Don Revie's Leeds he undoubtedly was, but Jack Charlton's most celebrated achievements came more recently across the Irish sea. Foreign managers taking control of other countries' national teams no longer raises eyebrows, but Charlton's appointment to the Republic of Ireland post was a revolutionary step.

Using the no-frills approach that had served him well in English club management, Charlton rebuilt the Irish team. Eschewing continental niceties for a long-ball style that was effective rather than pretty, and recruiting players through long-lost Irish family connections, he affected a dramatic turnaround in their international fortunes. The Republic qualified for the European Championships and the World Cup in 1988 and 1990 respectively. The World Cup in Italy was his finest hour, especially the penalty shoot-out victory over Romania that set up a quarter-final with Italy, bringing the nation to a standstill. The Republic's 1-0 defeat to the

◀ LEFT: Bobby Charlton.

Italians cemented his status as Ireland's second most popular icon after the Pope. USA 94 saw revenge against Italy, but Ireland's lack of imagination cost them. Imagination wasn't a word associated with him as a player either, but he stood tall against some of the best the game could throw at him.

see Bobby Charlton p. 154

▲ *ABOVE: Soccer veteran Jack Charlton.*

CHRISTIE, LINFORD (b. 1960)

Linford Christie is the best-ever European sprinter. His form in the early 1990s broke American dominance in the sprints. Prior to his win in the Barcelona Olympics in 1992, only four non-Americans had won the gold medal in 11 Olympics since World War II. Christie, the only European to have run under ten seconds, has won more major championship medals – 23 – than any other British male athlete. Until 1996, he remained unbeaten by a British athlete for eight years. Although he has never held the world record for the 100 m, his fastest time of 9.87 still stands as the European record.

Christie's record is matched by very few. But it was not until the early 1990s, that – already in his thirties – he produced his best form and was recognized as the supreme runner on both sides of the Atlantic. By 1993, Christie had won athletics' coveted Grand Slam, taking first place in the Commonwealth Games, European Champion-ships and World Championships. The biggest title of all, the Olympic title, came next. Aged 32, Christie was in the best form of his life. He had lost only once all season. His greatest threat seemed to come from the American Leroy Burrell, who had beaten him ten consecutive times. Christie beat Burrell in the quarter-finals only for Burrell to return the compliment in the semis. But in the final, Christie produced one of the performances of his life. After 60 m, he was clear of the field and pulled away to claim Britain's second 100-m gold medal in 12 years. Christie was the oldest man by four years to win the Olympic gold medal.

In Stuttgart in 1993, he completed the set. Lining up against his fiercest rivals, Christie again triumphed, taking the gold and setting his fastest-ever time. At the end of 1993, he was voted BBC Sports Personality of the Year. Although he was unable to retain the world

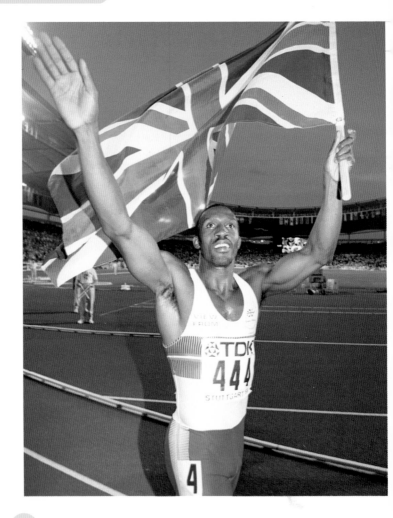

◀ LEFT: Britain's Linford Christie warming up at the 1993 World Championships in Stuttgart.

title in 1995, being hampered by a hamstring injury, or the Olympic title in 1996, when he false-started twice, he continues his involvement with athletics, training stars such as Jamie Baulch and Darren Campbell.

⟡ see Sebastian Coe p. 159

COE, SEBASTIAN (b. 1956)

The 800-m and 1500-m competitions in Moscow in 1980 were two of the most eagerly awaited races in athletics history. Brought together for the first time in two years were a pair of the greatest middle-distance runners the world had ever seen, Britain's Sebastian Coe and Steve Ovett. The two had dominated middle-distance running in the late 1970s and early 1980s, beating every other contender and smashing or equalling five world records between them in the run-up to Moscow. The last time they had met was in the 1978 European Championships, where their fear of each other had let in East Germany's Olaf Beyer to win the gold. Coe arrived in Moscow the hot favourite for the 800-m title, Ovett the slight favourite for the 1500 m.

Both qualified with ease for the final on 26 July. A slow first lap of 54.3 seconds saw both men floundering towards the back of the pack, waiting for one another to make the first move. With just 70 m left, Ovett flew past the Soviet Kirov and claimed the 800-m title. Coe, who took the silver, was shattered, saying afterwards that he had run the worst race of his life.

Six days later, though, Coe took his revenge. Once again, both men qualified for the final, but this time Ovett was the favourite at the longer distance. He had won 42 consecutive races at 1500 m and the mile since

1977. Coe's path was less smooth. He had struggled in his first-round heat and was now under even more media pressure to win the gold in his less favoured event. Between the British pair stood East Germany's Jürgen Straub, who led for most of the race. This time, though, Coe stayed near the front, anxious not to repeat his mistakes in the 800 m. On the final bend, he kicked for home and held off the challenge of both Straub and Ovett, who took the bronze.

see Linford Christie p. 157

▼ BELOW: Sebastian Coe in his victorious 1500-m race at the Moscow Olympics, 1980.

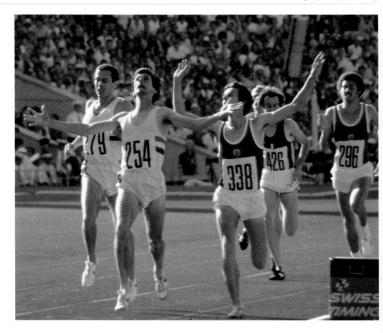

CRUYFF, JOHANN
(b. 1947)

Johann Cruyff's mother worked as a cleaner at Ajax's ground in Amsterdam, and the club were persuaded to give the youngster trials. One suspects they didn't regret it. He was fortunate to develop under the legendary Ajax coach Rinus Michels, but not as fortunate as Ajax were to have such an extraordinary talent born on their doorstep.

Cruyff had the lot: pace and strength allied to near-perfect ball control, and a punishing finish with either foot. The Ajax and Dutch teams of the early 1970s took the passing and movement of the 1950s Hungarian side into a new era. But, as is often the case with men of genius, Cruyff had a flawed side to his personality. An irritable and greedy nature saw him often at odds with authority and meant he was lost far too early to international football.

As a manager he was quixotic and opinionated too, and brought great success to Barcelona, landing them the coveted European Cup, but his

▲ *ABOVE: Great Dutch footballer Johann Cruyff.*

tenure at the Nou Camp was plagued by clashes with key players, notably Hristo Stoichkov and the Brazilian striker, Romario.

Despite his arrogance and irritability, Cruyff will be remembered as a breathtaking footballer to rank with the best in the world. Living in his native Holland, he has retired from management after developing a heart problem due to his penchant for chain-smoking.

⬛ *see* Eusébio p. 164

ERIKSSON, SVEN-GORAN (b. 1948)

Unassuming, softly spoken and seemingly dispassionate, Sven-Goran Eriksson has many qualities you would not expect to find in a football manager. He also possesses plenty of common sense, which appears to have stood him in good stead.

An unremarkable playing career was ended early by a knee injury; he then commenced a coaching career that has taken in a number of the biggest clubs in Europe and seen him collect an impressive list of national titles plus a smattering of European trophies.

Then the bombshell: for the first time in history, England appointed a foreigner as manager of the national team! Despite opposition from the sceptics – not all of them motivated by moronic nationalism – Eriksson quickly settled into his new role. Recognizing the talent available to him Eriksson set about organizing his players and, with improved tactics and discipline, virtually the same squad that lost at home to Germany in a World Cup qualifier under Kevin Keegan tore the Germans apart in the reverse fixture in Munich, winning 5-1 and sending a minor tremor through European football.

⬛ *see* David Beckham p. 145

▶ *RIGHT: England manager Sven-Goran Eriksson.*

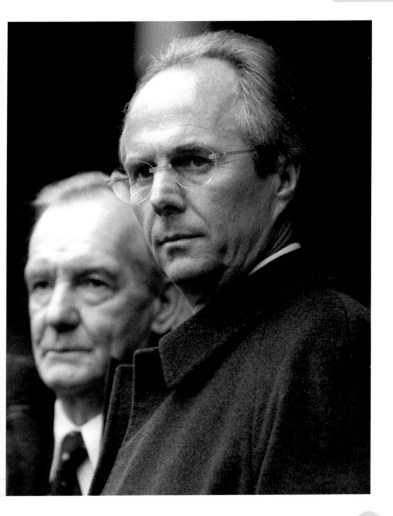

EUSÉBIO (b. 1942)

Mozambique-born Eusébio da Silva Ferreira was the first great African player and remains the continent's most famous footballing ambassador. His ability to run past players at pace, and hit fierce shots at speed, helped him maintain a goalscoring record so impressive that comparisons with Pelé are not inappropriate.

At Benfica, where he played most of his career, his goals tally was an unrivalled 316 from 294 games, and he appeared in four European Cup finals for the Lisbon club (sadly, winning only one).

English audiences warmed to Eusébio, having adopted him during the 1966 World Cup where, after North Korea had taken a 3-0 lead in the quarter-final, he hauled his side back into the game, scoring four as Portugal ran out 5–3 winners. The semi-final against England, where his duel with Nobby Stiles was the tournament's highlight, saw him in the role of gallant loser. His tears at the end of that Wembley clash were repeated at the same stadium two years later when Benfica lost out to Matt Busby's Manchester United in the European Cup Final, a match in which the 'Black Panther' had a chance to give his team the lead in the dying moments but shot straight at United's Alex Stepney. Despite his disappointment Eusébio turned to shake hands with Stepney and applaud the save.

◊ *see* Pelé p. 202

FANGIO, JUAN MANUEL (1911–95)

Juan Manuel Fangio was a noted Argentinean racing car driver and winner of the Formula One championship five times, including four in a row from 1954–57. He began his racing career in South America in 1934 and was Argentine National Champion in 1940 and 1941. The outbreak of World War II meant he did not begin racing in Europe until 1947. He won his first title in an Alfa Romeo in 1951. In 1954 he won his second title with Mercedes, taking eight out of 12 races. He won again with Mercedes the following year, but in 1955 the company withdrew from all racing following the disaster at Le Mans in which 81 spectators were killed. Fangio won his fourth title with Ferrari and his final title with Maserati. After his series of back-to-back championships, he retired in 1958 having won 24 Grand Prix in 51 starts.

◊ *see* Michael Schumacher p. 210

◄ *LEFT: African footballer Eusébio.*

FERGUSON, ALEX (b. 1941)

Ruthless as a player and driven as a manager, Alex Ferguson's record is one that only Bob Paisley can match. His background from the school of hard knocks in Govan served him well, requiring a commitment and self-discipline that he has always demanded, and received, from his players. Strange that such a professional started his footballing life with archetypal amateurs Queen's Park, but it was as Aberdeen manager that he really made his mark. For six years the Old Firm dominance was interrupted as three titles and a European trophy arrived at Pittodrie. Manchester United, desperate to escape Liverpool's shadow, broke the bank, and Aberdonian hearts, to get their man. Although his 15-year tenure is the Premiership's longest and Ferguson's position is now unassailable, the first trophy did not arrive for four years amid mutterings that the Midas touch had vanished.

However, since landing United's first title in 26 years, the only competition has been for second place. Although he was widely expected to retire at the end of the 2002 season, Ferguson, apparently at the suggestion of his wife, surprised everyone by agreeing to a new contract to stay on as manager.

◨ see Matt Busby p. 150

▶ RIGHT: Manchester United manager Sir Alex Ferguson.

FOREMAN, GEORGE (b. 1948)

George Foreman, born into poverty in Texas in 1948, was, at just under 2 m (6 ft 4 in), a giant of a boxer. Although he dropped out of school at 14, it was not until he was 18 that he first put on a pair of boxing gloves. Winning the Olympic heavyweight title in 1968, he turned professional in 1969 and won all of the 38 fights he had before his 1973 meeting with Joe Frazier.

Frazier, who had held the world title since 1968, had also been the Olympic champion in 1964. Despite being physically a smaller man, he had the advantage of experience, and with Foreman rated at 3–1 was very much favourite to win. The fight took place at the National Stadium in Kingston, Jamaica. As soon as the bell sounded for the first round, Frazier came bounding out of his corner just as he always did. Foreman simply stood his ground, and an enormous fight erupted in the centre of the ring. Frazier, who had a distinct disadvantage in reach, tried to punch his way towards Foreman, but was kept at bay by a constant barrage of long punches. Foreman then appeared to take deliberate aim with a clubbing right which smashed into Frazier's jaw and sent him to the canvas. Frazier rose on two, but looked distinctly wobbly for the standing eight count. Seemingly unaffected, Frazier pushed forward again and caught Foreman with a few hard blows, but with apparently no effect on the giant Texan. The round finally came to an end with Foreman very much on top.

The second round commenced much as the first had. Frazier exploded out of his corner, but managed only to tumble straight into a stinging two-punch combination which again sent him on to the deck. This time, he stayed there for all of the eight count. From then on, he was in a daze; unaware of what was going on, he was sent to the ground for a fifth time. Battered and bleeding, Joe Frazier had become a pathetic sight.

By now, even Foreman was begging Frazier to stay down, but despite all this he somehow managed to drag himself to his feet for the sixth time, though mercifully the referee stopped the fight just 35 seconds later. It was just 1 minute 35 seconds into the second round! After the fight was over, Frazier made what must be one of the biggest under-statements ever in boxing: 'We were fooled into thinking it would be easy.... I guess we underrated him'. Both fighters' careers continued. Foreman held the world title for just over 18 months.

◄ see Mohammed Ali p. 134

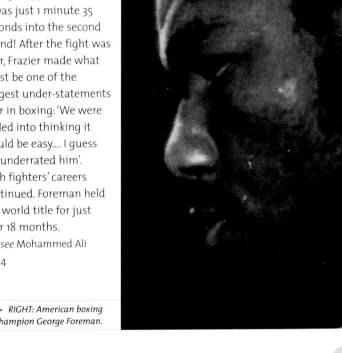

▶ RIGHT: American boxing champion George Foreman.

GARRINCHA (b. 1933)

Manuel dos Santos Francisco, otherwise known as Garrincha, was like a character from a fairytale. Born into poverty, and with a disability that meant his legs were bowed in opposite directions, he somehow managed to become one of the most feared attackers in the history of the game.

▲ ABOVE: Garrincha, one of the greatest players in the history of Brazilian football.

Great balance and superb close control made him a deadly dribbler, and he was the first of the great Brazilian players to perfect the 'banana' shot.

He was 24 before he forced his way into the national side, but his exploits in three World Cups, particularly the successful 1958 and 1962 campaigns, earned him his place in Brazilian folklore. Perhaps his greatest moment was in 1962 when, after Pelé had bowed out of the tournament with an injury, he took on the responsibility of leading the Brazilian attack. Garrincha destroyed England in the quarter-finals, then did the same to the violent hosts Chile in the semis and, despite his sending-off late in that game, he was allowed to appear in the final where he collected his second winner's medal. Unlike most modern Brazilian players, Garrincha played his domestic football in his home country, notably with Botafogo, whose rivalry with Pelé's Santos was a feature of the era.

⬥ see Pelé p. 202

GRAF, STEFFI (b. 1969)

German tennis player Steffi Graf first came to prominence in 1984, when she won the demonstration event at the Olympic Games. Graf won the gold medal when tennis returned as a full-scale Olympic sport at the next Games, in Seoul in 1988. The same year, she claimed all four titles in the tennis Grand Slam. This achievement, combined with her Olympic medal, was called the 'Golden Slam'. Graf had power, pace and accuracy and she was able to intimidate other players after building up a remarkable record of success. Before she retired in 1999, at the end of a 15-year career, she won 22 Grand Slam titles and 85 other tournaments. In 2001, Graf married another prominent tennis champion, André Agassi.

⬥ see Andre Agassi p. 134

HENRY, THIERRY (b. 1977)

When the troublesome
and disruptive Nicolas
Anelka left Arsenal in
1998, Arsène Wenger
turned to another quick
French attacker to
replace him. Thierry
Henry had emerged as a
wide attacking player at
Monaco under Wenger's
tutelage, and won a
league title there in
1998. A lucrative move to
Juventus followed, but,
like many others in Serie
A, Henry spent more
time on the bench than
the pitch, and left after
less than a year. He
had a difficult start at
Arsenal, when both manager and player seemed unsure as to the most
satisfactory use for all that skill and speed. Only when Wenger
consistently used Henry in a central striking role, an opportunity afforded
by Dennis Bergkamp's injuries and loss of form, was his true potential
unearthed. Henry's second and third seasons at Arsenal brought him a
torrent of goals in a classy side. The discovery that he could play as an

orthodox front man was of equal benefit to France, for whom the addition of a world-class striker proved to be the missing piece in their attacking jigsaw.

The 2002 World Cup suggested Henry still has much to prove as an international player, but his subsequent league form in 2002/3 proved little short of sensational.

◆ see David Beckham p. 145

HURST, GEOFF (b. 1941)

The sight of an airborne Geoff Hurst smashing his hat-trick to seal England's World Cup Final victory is one of the country's indelible post-war images. Inevitably, it dwarfed the rest of his career, but at the beginning of the tournament Hurst was a squad player, drafted in by Sir Alf Ramsey merely as cover for the more experienced Roger Hunt and Jimmy Greaves (Hurst had only made his debut for England earlier that year). But an injury to Greaves in the group stage provided Hurst with his opportunity. It was one he seized, scoring the only goal against Argentina in the quarter-finals.

Hurst was groomed as a striker by Ron Greenwood at West Ham; along with England team-mates Martin Peters and skipper Bobby Moore, he was a graduate of the Upton Park academy. After tasting the ultimate success at 24, Hurst's career rather stagnated and by the time he left the Hammers for Stoke at the age of 30 it was all but over. Like nearly all the 1966 England team, he was a managerial failure and excused himself from football for 15 years before returning as a promotional figurehead for England's successful Euro 96 bid. More recently he was part of the team that fought Germany for the right to host the 2006 World Cup Finals. On this occasion he lost. (*See over for illustration.*)

◆ see Bobby Charlton p. 154

JOHNSON, MICHAEL (b. 1967)

Michael Johnson – 'Superman' – is the fastest man in the world over 200 m and 400 m, a double Olympic champion, triple world champion, and double world-record holder, his supremacy is unquestioned. His unique running style, that seems to break every rule in the book, making him appear as if he is running leaning back, makes him an even more fascinating performer.

Currently, he is arguably the world's best-known athlete and certainly track-and-field's biggest draw. This claim is borne out by the events of the 1997 World Championships held in Athens and Johnson's controversial appearance there. The 30-year-old from Dallas, Texas, had not been selected for the American team, after injury had forced him to withdraw from the US trials in Indianapolis, Indiana. The strict American qualifying rules, which decree that only the first three in the trials qualify for the championships, left Johnson out of the team and the world without one of its biggest athletes at one of its biggest tournaments. He was given a wild-card entry to the championships to run the 400-m event.

Despite almost failing to qualify in one of the heats Johnson defended his title successfully. He won the final in a time of 44.12 seconds, passing the Ugandan athlete Davis Kamoga, who led for much of the race and who clocked 44.37 seconds. Johnson, the man who had not qualified for the US team, was now the world champion for the second time. This performance came just a year after two world-record runs at the Atlanta Olympics, when he took the gold medal in both the 200 m and 400 m. (*See over for illustration.*)

◆ see Jesse Owens p. 200

◀ *LEFT: England hat-trick scorer Geoff Hurst*

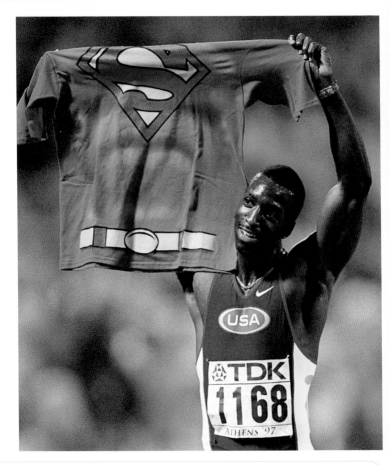

▲ *ABOVE: Michael Johnson showing off his Superman shirt at the 1997 World Championships in Athens.*

▶ RIGHT: Former England manager Kevin Keegan

KEEGAN, KEVIN (b. 1951)

Hugely committed, deeply passionate – and, at times, comically naive – Kevin Keegan is one of the great characters of the modern game. Plucked from obscurity at Scunthorpe by Bill Shankly, Keegan became the focal point of Liverpool's attack, and his almost telepathic understanding with John Toshack proved to be one of the club's most successful striking partnerships. Never afraid of a new challenge, Keegan later moved to Hamburg, where his enthusiasm won colleagues and fans over after a shaky start. Then it was back to England and another successful spell at Southampton under Lawrie McMenemy, and a final flourish at Newcastle.

Twenty-one goals in 63 internationals was a decent return for a striker, but Keegan rarely got the opportunity to shine in major tournaments – a 20-minute stint as a substitute against Spain in 1982 was his only appearance at a World Cup finals.

As a club manager Keegan has always sent out teams with one objective in mind: to attack. This approach has made his teams popular but has not seen him collect any major silverware. He was an absurd choice as England manager, clearly lacking the tactical wherewithal for international football, but he does deserve credit for reviving the fortunes of Newcastle, Fulham and Manchester City.

◆ see Sven-Goran Eriksson p. 162

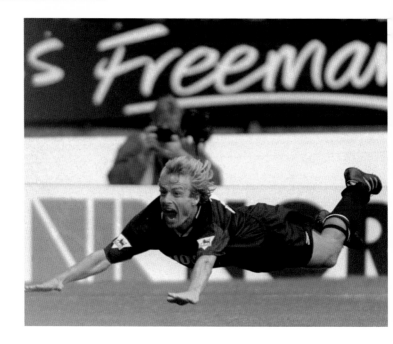

KLINSMANN, JURGEN (b. 1964)

Jurgen Klinsmann has always been keen to embrace new challenges, and when he returned to Tottenham Hotspur for a second spell in December 1997 he faced one of his biggest. Under the inept management of Christian Gross, an unpopular appointment by an unpopular chairman, Alan Sugar, the club were facing relegation. That they avoided this fate was largely down to the German striker who, repeating his success of the 1994/95 season, lit up White Hart Lane with his leggy athleticism and, more crucially, goals.

◀ *LEFT: German soccer star Jurgen Klinsmann.*

Klinsmann's appetite for new adventures is evidenced by his willingness to play in Italy, France and England, as well as his native Germany. Quick and incisive in the box, as well as good in the air, Klinsmann has been a consistent goal scorer at every one of his clubs, even maintaining an impressive ratio in the notoriously defensive Serie A with Inter. Adaptable and intelligent (while at Spurs he spoke English more eloquently than most of his colleagues), he appeared in three World Cups, scoring 11 goals in 17 games. Sometimes criticized for diving, it was a foul on him that won the penalty from which Andreas Brehme scored to win the 1990 World Cup Final for Germany.

◆ *see* Franz Beckenbauer p. 141

KORBUT, OLGA VALENTINOVA (b. 1955)

Olga Valentinova Korbut, a 1.5-m (4-ft 11-in), 37.8-kg (6-stone) gymnast from Grodno in Belarus, so captured the public's imagination that she instantly became a superstar. There were many reasons for Korbut's immense popularity. There were the tears she spilt after failure on the bars in the all-round competition meant that she had lost her chance of a gold medal at the Munich Olympics. Then there were her innocent, stylish performances on the floor, which contrasted greatly with those of many of her compatriots. Finally, there was her appearance – 17 going on 12. Korbut was dubbed the 'Munich Munchkin'.

Korbut had already claimed gold in the team event by the time the individual events began. Halfway through the all-round event, she was in the lead and threatening the favourite, Tourischeva, as she went to her next piece of apparatus, the asymmetric bars. But then disaster struck. She scuffed her mount, slipped off the bars and fluffed a simple remount.

Korbut was given the lowly mark of 7.5, destroying her chances of victory. Immediately, she burst into tears, a scene which was picked up by the TV cameras and which endeared her to the public even more. Two days later, Korbut reappeared in the individual events to claim two golds, one for the balance beam and the other for the floor exercise, at which she excelled with her dazzling display of somersaults, showbiz, and smiles. She also won a silver medal on the asymmetric bars. Munich launched Korbut's career, and

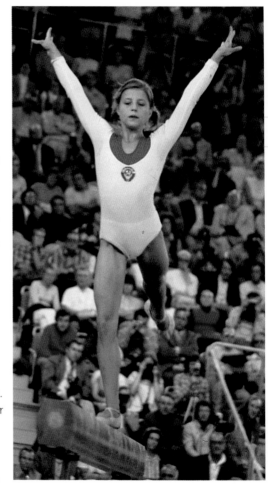

she went on to become the first-ever gymnast to do a back somersault on the beam. She later married a Belarussian singer and was living in Grodno, near Chernobyl, when the nuclear tragedy struck in 1986. Korbut moved to Atlanta, Georgia, and established a foundation for Chernobyl victims.

◆ see Ellen MacArthur p. 187

◀ LEFT: Olga Korbut, the 'Munich Munchkin' at the 1972 Olympics, where she became an instant and much-adored celebrity.

LARA, BRIAN (b. 1969)

In April 2004, a small, young, left-handed batsman from Trinidad set about rewriting the record books – again. Ten years earlier, on 18 April 1994 in the fifth Test against England at the Recreation Ground, St Johns, Antigua, Lara broke Sir Gary Sobers long-standing Test record by scoring 375 runs. On 6 June that year, he also broke the world record for the highest number of runs scored in a first-class match when he hit 501 not out for Warwickshire against Durham. Lara became only the second man in history to hold both records at the same time. His Test Match record was finally broken by Australian batsman Matthew Hayden, who scored 380 runs against Zimbabwe in October 2003. But Lara dramatically reclaimed his Test Match record by scoring an extraordinary 400 not out against England on 12 April 2004 at the same ground in Antigua where he first broke the record.

Aged just 20, Lara had made his Test debut against Pakistan in December 1990, scoring 44 in his first Test innings. By the time England arrived in the Caribbean four years later, his Test average was up to 53.69. Before that series, he had stated his aim to score a triple century. This he rapidly did, breaking a 36-year-old world record in the process. This instantly elevated Lara to the status of national hero, but a period of mixed fortunes for the West Indies team under his leadership led many to question his skills. These doubts were thoroughly laid to rest with his triumphant performance in 2004, however, in an innings that saw him regain his hero status once and for all. Lara faced 582 deliveries and hit 43 fours and four sixes in a textbook innings, finally declaring on 400. He is truly one of the greatest cricketers of all time.

◊ *see* Ian Botham p. 147

▶ *RIGHT: Brian Lara walks off the pitch through a triumphal arch of bats and stumps.*

LAW, DENIS (b. 1940)

He squinted, was scrawny and his unkempt, spiky hair gave him the appearance of a toilet brush. Yet, all this appeared little hindrance to Denis Law, who emerged as one of Manchester United's and Scotland's finest-ever strikers. The 'flying Scot' was as quick as a greyhound.

He owes a huge debt to Bill Shankly, his first manager at Huddersfield, who moulded a novice schoolboy into an 18-year-old international. Like Jimmy Greaves, he failed to settle in Italy and it was only his return to Manchester, swapping a blue shirt for a red one, that revived his career. His forward combination with George Best and Bobby Charlton was the finest in English club football. Law left Old Trafford after being kicked out of the club by Tommy Docherty who made an example of him. Law joined Man City and came back to haunt Docherty the following season when his back-heeled goal for City in the Manchester derby contributed to United's relegation to Division Two. Famously, Law did not celebrate the goal. Head bowed, he simply turned round and walked solemnly back to the centre-circle. Since his retirement, his partnership with former team-mate Paddy Crerand has made him one of the circuit's most popular after-dinner speakers.

see George Best p. 145

LEWIS, CARL (b. 1961)

Frederick Carlton Lewis is an American sprinter and jumper, born in Birmingham, Alabama. A star in high school and at the University of Houston, he became possibly the greatest track athlete of all time. After winning three gold medals at the World Championships in Helsinki in 1983, he went on at the 1984 Summer Olympics to match Jesse Owens' record by winning four gold medals (the 100-m and 200-m sprints, the

▶ RIGHT: Scottish soccer star Denis Law.

long jump and the 4 x 100 m relay). He also won three medals – two gold and one silver – at the 1988 Olympics, two gold again in 1992, and another gold in 1996, equalling the record for most gold medals overall. He retired in 1997.

see Jesse Owens p. 200

LINEKER, GARY (b. 1960)

English footballer Lineker is a man it is hard to dislike, even if you find his personality a little anodyne. A model professional with all his clubs, not a season went by without Lineker delivering his quota of goals; he was top scorer in England three times, each time with different clubs. Despite recent gags regarding a longstanding toe problem, Lineker was rarely injured until moving to Japan and, incredibly for a player who regularly suffered intense provocation, went through his entire career without receiving a yellow card.

Following success in England with Leicester and Everton, Lineker moved to Barcelona, and soon proved he was capable of rising to the challenges of life in a foreign country. Indeed, but for a disagreement with Johan Cruyff who, bafflingly, decided that Lineker's best position was on the right wing, he could well have spent the rest of his career at the Nou Camp. As it was he returned to England to play for Terry Venables at Spurs with whom, at the age of 30, he finally collected his first domestic trophy, the FA Cup in 1991.

Since retiring, Lineker has enjoyed a successful media career, succeeding Des Lynam as the anchor on *Match of the Day*. He had an outstanding 2002 World Cup in this capacity.

see Alan Shearer p. 213

▶ *RIGHT: Soccer's Mr Nice Guy Gary Lineker.*

MACARTHUR, ELLEN (b. 1976)

At the age of 26, Ellen MacArthur finshed yachting's toughest race, the Vendee Globe, and became the youngest person ever to complete the race and the fastest women ever to circumnavigate the globe. From the land-locked county of Derbyshire, England, Ellen's passionate relationship with sailing began when she was eight and stepped aboard her aunt's boat to go sailing on the east coast. She saved up her school dinner

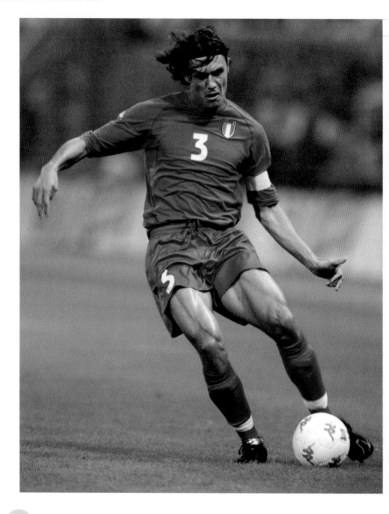

◀ *LEFT: Paolo Maldini.*

money for three years to buy her first boat – an 8-ft dinghy. At the age of 18 she sailed alone around Britain and won the BT/YJA Young Sailor of the Year. Such tenacity and determination at such a young age has made her a national heroine and will undoubtedly ensure even greater achievements.

◆ *see* Olga Valentinova Korbut p. 179

MALDINI, PAOLO (b. 1968)

Arguably the finest left-back ever to play the game, Paolo Maldini's class was emphasized early when, at 16, he became one of Serie A's youngest-ever debutants in 1985. Accomplished on the ball and decisive in the tackle, Maldini has been the immovable object of world football, equally comfortable on the left or in the centre.

Unusually for someone who could have commanded huge signing-on fees, he has played his club football only with Milan. His six league titles, four Italian Cups and three European Cups are a deserving reflection of his talent and loyalty.

Ultimate international success continues to elude Maldini, though. He was a member of the Italian teams that failed to secure the world crown at Italia 90, USA 94 and France 98, each time going out on penalties (most crushingly in 1994 when they were beaten by Brazil in the final). Maldini has played in some of the tightest defences the game has known, the foursome he made up with Antonio Benarrivo, Franco Baresi and Alessandro Costacurta in USA 94 being perhaps the finest of all. In 2003 he lifted the European Cup at Old Trafford as Milan's captain. Father Cesare performed the same task for the same club in the same country 40 years earlier.

◆ *see* David Beckham p. 145

MARADONA, DIEGO (b. 1960)

The most naturally gifted player football has ever seen, or a despicable drug-ridden cheat? Whatever your opinion, Maradona's talent was undeniable. After emerging in his native Argentina with Argentinos Juniors, for whom he made his league debut aged only 15, Maradona quickly attracted the attention of European scouts.

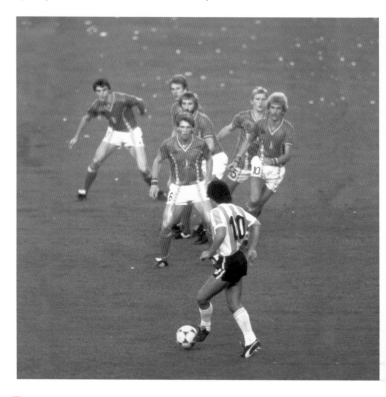

A move to Spain for £4.2 million should have made him the jewel in Barcelona's star-studded crown, but the young and immature Diego failed to settle and joined Napoli in Italy's Serie A for £6.9 million. Maradona brought unprecedented success to Naples, single-handedly shifting the powerbase of Italian football from north to south, but he also fell in with the wrong crowd. Throughout his time there he was repeatedly seen in the company of local mobsters, and rumours of cocaine addiction were rife.

The 1986 World Cup quarter-final versus England provided an insight to his personality: a flagrant punch past Peter Shilton for Argentina's first goal was followed by a 60-yard run and wonder-goal minutes later.

Maradona's personal flaws make him an unattractive figure, but should not obscure his vast talents as a footballer. His poor origins and volatility made him susceptible to bad advice off the pitch and provocation on it, compounded by his failure to ignore either.

see Pelé p. 202

MARCIANO, ROCKY (1923–69)

Rocky Marciano, whose real name was Rocco Francis Marchegiano, was the undefeated heavyweight champion of the world between 1952, when he knocked out the reigning champion, Jersey Joe Walcott. Marciano had come to attention a year before, in 1951, when he defeated a former world champion, Joe Louis, the 'Brown Bomber'. Marciano took up boxing while serving in the US forces in Britain during World War II and turned professional in 1947. Known as the 'Brockton Blockbuster' after the Massachusetts town where he was born, Marciano won 49 professional boxing matches, which still remains a record.

see Mohammed Ali p. 134

◀ *LEFT: Maradona snakecharms the Belgians during the 1982 World Cup in Spain.*

MATTHEWS, STANLEY (1915–2000)

Stanley Matthews became known as the 'Wizard of Dribble' for his remarkable ability to advance the ball by small touches of the foot. Matthews was also known as the 'First Gentleman of Soccer' for his sportsmanship even though, in 1968, while acting as a club manager, he was reprimanded for giving new players illegal signing bonuses and incentive payments for winning. As a footballer, Matthews built up an impressive statistical record. He played for England in 54 international matches, was twice named Footballer of the Year and won the first European Footballer of the Year award in 1956. Matthews was still playing first-class football at the age of 50, the same year he was awarded a knighthood. In 1990, he became chairman of his old club, Stoke City.

◆ see Geoff Hurst p. 173

McENROE, JOHN (b. 1959)

The American John McEnroe was among the most brilliant natural talents to appear on a tennis court. He excelled at surprising opponents by skilful use of disguise to place the ball in out-of-reach places on court. McEnroe came to notice in 1977, as an 18-year-old qualifier, when he unexpectedly reached the semi-finals at Wimbledon. McEnroe won seven Grand Slam singles titles (Wimbledon 1981, 1983, 1984 and the US Open 1979, 1980, 1981, 1984) and eight doubles, together with 68 other singles and 44 other doubles titles. He was, however, a controversial player due to his inability to control his temper during matches. He frequently insulted and intimidated referees and was suspected of using arguments and delays to upset his opponents' concentration. (*See over for illustration.*)

◆ see Boris Becker p. 143

◄ *LEFT: The 'Wizard of Dribble', Stanley Matthews.*

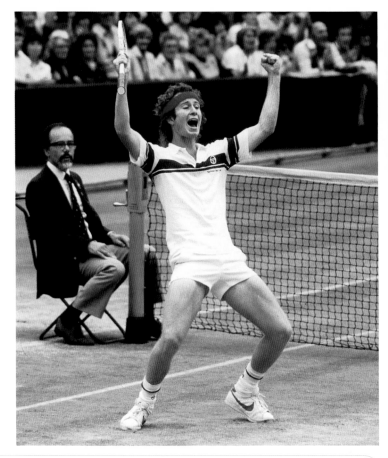

▲ *ABOVE: A jubilant John McEnroe after beating hot favourite Bjorn Borg for the men's singles title at Wimbledon, 1981.*

MOORE, BOBBY (1959–93)

English footballer Bobby Moore was the ultimate example of mind over body. He appeared to possess few of the physical attributes required in a great defender, but made up for his lack of muscle with an ability to read the game that bordered on the psychic. Moore took the ball by stealth

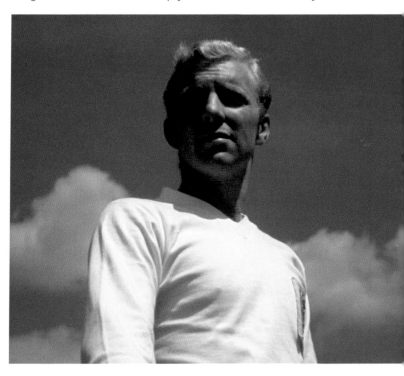

▲ *ABOVE: Bobby Moore.*

▶ RIGHT: German powerhouse Gerd Müller.

rather than power and, though he rarely needed to resort to tackling, when he did so it was always surgical and clean. Rattling bones wasn't his style. He was loyal too; with the exception of a swansong alongside George Best and Rodney Marsh at Fulham, Moore spent his entire career at West Ham. Upton Park now has a stand named after him, and the ground is home to a bust and plaque honouring his achievements.

His England career started in 1962, and continued almost unbroken until his retirement from internationals in 1973. He competed in three World Cups, winning the Player of the Tournament award in 1966 when he captained England to a 4-2 victory over Germany in the final.

◆ see George Best p. 145

MÜLLER, GERD (b. 1945)

Gerd Müller, 'Der Bomber,' was arguably the most lethal finisher in the history of the game. Like many out-and-out goalscorers, he did little outside the penalty area, and looked unremarkable in open play, but in the box his reflexes were cobra-like. Powerful, and with terrific balance, he was always in the right position to receive the ball, his body always shaped in readiness for a strike on goal.

Müller was drafted into the German team in 1966 immediately after the World Cup final, and surprisingly retired after scoring the winner against Holland in the 1974 final, aged only 28. The eight years in between were a one-man goal-fest as Germany swept aside lesser opposition, and even proved themselves a match for the inspired Dutch. At club level Müller spent 15 years with Bayern Munich, scoring at a ratio of better than one goal per game for a remarkable seven seasons.

◆ see Franz Beckenbauer p. 141

NAVRATILOVA, MARTINA (b. 1956)

Born in communist-ruled Czechoslovakia, Martina Navratilova defected to the US in 1975 and became a US citizen in 1981. Widely considered the greatest female tennis player of the twentieth century, Navratilova was the first to include special diet and exercise in her training programme. Her career lasted from 1973 to 1994 and included a 16-year friendly rivalry with the US player Chris Evert: they contested no less than 65 tournament finals. Although Navratilova never won a true Grand Slam, which has to be achieved within a single year, she held all four of these prime tournaments at the same time, between May 1983 and January 1984. In all, Navratilova won 167 singles and 171 doubles tournaments. She also claimed a total of 58 Grand Slam titles comprising 18 singles, eight mixed doubles and 32 doubles, the last of them in the Australian Open in 2003, when she was aged 46.

◆ *see* Steffi Graf p. 171

▼ *BELOW: A beaming Navratilova holding up the women's singles title shield, 1990.*

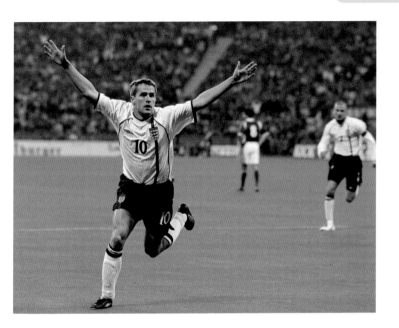

OWEN, MICHAEL (b. 1979)

Few footballers achieve in a lifetime what Michael Owen had achieved by the age of 22. At 17 years and 144 days he became the youngest player ever to appear in the Liverpool first team, then followed that by becoming the youngest England player of the twentieth century. By the time he was 18 he was a world star, largely on account of his exploits at France 98 where, against Argentina in the second round, he scored one of the greatest World Cup goals of all time.

▲ *ABOVE: A young Michael Owen celebrates a goal.*

Having spent two years learning to live with vulnerable hamstrings, Owen re-emerged late in the 2000/01 season to lead the Liverpool line as they won a unique treble of cups. His performance in the FA Cup Final, when he scored both goals in Liverpool's 2-1 defeat of Arsenal, was probably his best, but it was his consistency over this period that most impressed.

Owen's principal asset is his blistering pace, but to dismiss him as merely a speed-merchant would be to take him lightly. He is able to use either foot, has a good first touch, good balance, and takes a high percentage of his chances. He scored his 100th Premiership goal in April 2003, a remarkable achievement for a 22-year-old.

⟳ see David Beckham p. 145

OWENS, JESSE (1913–80)

Jesse Owens is one of the most famous sportsmen of the century, a symbol of both supreme athleticism and the struggle against racism and bigotry everywhere. His finest hour was at the 1936 Berlin Olympics, where he won four gold medals, triumphing in the 100 and 200 m, the 4 x 100-m relay, and the long jump. Nazi leader Adolf Hitler, however, refused to shake Owens' hand or present him with his medals. Hitler's handshake would have been superfluous in any case. His disdain of Owens' achievements makes them stand as one of the greatest sporting stories of the century.

Born in Alabama in 1913, James 'Jesse' Cleveland Owens dominated the sprint distances in the 1930s. His stature as a world-class athlete was confirmed in 1935, when he broke five world records and equalled a sixth in the space of 45 minutes while competing at the Big Ten Championships in Michigan. Starting at 3.15 pm, Owens equalled the 100-yd-dash world record and beat the long jump, 220-yd dash, 200-m dash, and 220-yd low hurdles. En route, he smashed the 200-m-hurdles record. His long-jump record was to stand until 1960. Not bad for someone who smoked 35 cigarettes a day.

■ *see* Linford Christie p. 157

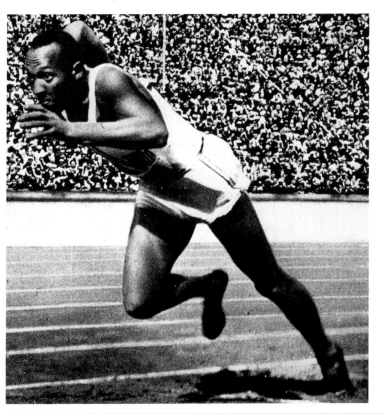

▲ *ABOVE: US athlete Jesse Owens, star of the 1936 Olympics.*

PELÉ (b. 1940)

Edson Arantes di Nascimento is the greatest footballer of all time. Born in Tes Coracoes, a small provincial town in the Brazilian state of Minas Gerais, Pelé (as he is better known) began his career at Santos, forcing his way into the first team by the age of 16, and made his debut for Brazil a year later in 1958 when, at 17, he collected his first World Cup winner's medal in Sweden. Pelé went on to play in three more World Cup tournaments; he struggled with injuries in 1962, and again in 1966, but in 1970, playing in a deeper role, he was the architect of some of the finest football the game has ever known. Surrounded by players who were in tune with his alert mind and quick feet, Brazil produced unforgettable, almost perfect football.

Pelé played all his domestic football in his beloved white shirt for Santos, a career that spanned nearly 20 years. He retired in 1974, but was persuaded to return to the game a year later when, like Franz Beckenbauer, Bobby Moore and many other of his old adversaries, he signed a $4.5 million contract to play in the newly-formed NASL with New York Cosmos. Pelé has remained in football as an ambassador for the game, and has served a spell as Brazil's Minister for Sport.

◼ see Diego Maradona p. 190

PLATINI, MICHEL (b. 1955)

The finest European midfielder of the past 30 years, Michel Platini combined sublime skill with a goalscoring record that would put many international forwards to shame. Touch, vision and great accuracy with either foot made him a divine playmaker, but he added the virtue of a constant flow of goals, both from set-pieces and open play. After ten years in the French league, he turned down a move to Arsenal in 1982 claiming, perhaps justifiably, that English clubs played too many games. The Gunners' loss was Juventus' gain, as trophies followed for the Italian giants. Platini's high point came in the 1984 European Championships when, teaming up with Jean Tigana and Alain Giresse in midfield, he skippered France to a famous victory on home soil. Platini's astonishing return of nine goals in five games, including two hat-tricks, made him the tournament's top scorer. His business interests brought about a shock retirement in 1987, but he was tempted by the French national manager's job three years later.

An uneasy tenure, Platini resigned after France's premature exit from Euro 92 but became president of the France 98 World Cup committee and continues to enjoy a high profile as a special advisor to FIFA.

◆ *see* Sven-Goran Eriksson p. 162

▼ BELOW: *Mexico, 1986. Platini scores against Brazil in the World Cup quarter-final.*

RONALDO (b. 1976)

It was clear from an early age that Ronaldo Luis Nazario de Lima had the lot. Playing in Brazilian football as a teenager he proved unstoppable, and was promptly shipped off to Europe to play for PSV Eindhoven in Holland.

In Europe he has torn apart Dutch, Spanish and Italian club defences with equal relish, and had a brilliant Copa América with Brazil in 1997. He came into the 1998 World Cup billed as the world's greatest player and lived up to the hype with some fine performances, but the events surrounding his 'funny turn' prior to the final against France (and his subsequent insipid performance) meant fans came away discussing his health rather than his football. Not any more. The Golden Boot in Japan and Korea in the World Cup Finals in 2002 confirmed that the comeback kid had truly returned.

see Pelé p. 202

▶ RIGHT: Ronaldo.

SAMPRAS, PETE (b. 1971)

The American Pete Sampras was only 28 days past his 19th birthday when he was able to produce and sustain a display of classic elegance and power to become the youngest winner of the US Open in New York and, with a ranking of 12, the lowest seed to win the championships since 1966. Sampras had spent numerous hours of his life watching tapes of his tennis idols, Rod Laver and Ken Rosewall.

As the tournament progressed, Sampras showed increasing maturity as his count of service aces moved towards the 100 mark. In the final, he faced the other American tennis sensation and his great rival, André Agassi. Agassi's volatility and swashbuckling tennis had taken some of the shine off Sampras's displays, but the final revealed the better player as Sampras destroyed his opponent 6–4, 6–3, 6–2 with an awesome display.

The tall Californian played textbook tennis as Agassi was completely overwhelmed in a mere hour and 42 minutes. He was only able to salvage eight points on the Sampras serve in the first two sets. A bemused Agassi described the defeat as 'an old-fashioned street mugging. I had my backside kicked. Everything he touched turned to gold. The way he played he should come back to Vegas with me and play the casinos'.

Like Agassi, Sampras was completely awestruck by his own performance. 'This is ultimate tennis. Whatever I do in the rest of my career I will always be the US Open champion,' he said.

see André Agassi p. 134

◀ *LEFT: 19-year-old Pete Sampras playing against compatriot André Agassi at the 1990 US Open.*

SCHMEICHEL, PETER (b. 1963)

Of all Sir Alex Ferguson's signings as a manager, few were as shrewd as his capture in 1991 of goalkeeping giant Peter Schmeichel. (Knowing what they know now Brondby would surely have charged and received 30 times the £500,000 fee they asked United to cough up for the great Dane.) A giant presence between the sticks, Schmeichel's arrival provided a defensive platform that launched United on a decade of dominance. Though famous for bellowing vocal 'encouragement' to his team-mates – outbursts to match even the hair-drying performances of his manager – he was far more than just a big gob. His starfish presence shrank the goal for any onrushing forward and made him the best one-on-one keeper in the world (some would say of all time), while his last-gasp charges into the opposing penalty area started a trend and brought him a European goal. The burdens of United's year-round schedule saw him depart at the top, weeks after winning the treble, but retirement was a long way off for this enthusiastic fitness fanatic. A surprise return to the Premiership has seen him past his best at Aston Villa, but the void left by his departure at Old Trafford has never been truly filled. The sight of him at Maine Road in 2002/03 was a strange one for United fans. He finally retired in May 2003.

◆ see David Seaman p. 210

▶ RIGHT: Goalkeeping legend Peter Schmeichel.

SCHUMACHER, MICHAEL (b. 1969)

Michael Schumacher, born in Hurth, Germany, is the world's most successful Formula One driver. He made his debut in 1991 as a fill-in driver for Jordan. He was then signed by Benetton-Ford for his next race, and quickly showed potential. In 1994 he won the championship for Benetton and again the following year. He signed a contract with Ferrari for 1996 and in the 2000 season he won the first drivers' title for Ferrari since 1979. The next year, on the way to his fourth title, he broke Alain Prost's record for the most wins. In a dominant 2002, he easily took his fifth world title, equalling the record set by Juan Manuel Fangio. In 2003 he topped that record by winning the F1 championship title for the sixth time in a very close season. As yet, his domination shows no sign of waning.

◆ see Ayrton Senna p. 212

SEAMAN, DAVID (b. 1963)

David Seaman cost Arsenal £1.3 million from QPR in 1990. Perhaps not a bargain on the same scale as Alex Ferguson's swoop for Peter Schmeichel, but not a bad bit of business. Since joining the Gunners, Seaman has helped the club to a succession of trophies, including League and Cup doubles in 1998 and 2002.

A usually reliable keeper, Seaman has been harshly pilloried for a couple of high-profile errors; in the 1995 European Cup Winners' Cup Final he was lobbed by Real Zaragoza's Nayim from the half-way line and, against Germany in a World Cup qualifier in 2000, he was beaten from 35 yards by a Dietmar Hamann free-kick. But those who criticize

▶ RIGHT: England goalkeeper David Seaman.

him for this conveniently forget the countless hours of impeccable service he has given both Arsenal and England. Seaman has been England's number one for most of the last ten years, a period in which only Tim Flowers and Nigel Martyn have seriously threatened to displace him. Seaman was outstanding at Euro 96, France 98 and the 2002 World Cup Finals despite his over-publicised mistake against Brazil. His fantastic, last-minute save in the 2003 FA Cup semi-final was the perfect riposte to critics who thought he was past his best.

◆ see Peter Shilton p. 213

SENNA, AYRTON (1960–94)

Ayrton Senna da Silva won the Formual One title three times. Born in Sao Paulo, Brazil, he was encouraged by his father and got behind the wheel of his first kart at the age of four. He arrived in Europe in 1981 and progressed through competition until he secured a seat with the Toleman-Hart F1 team. The next year, Senna joined the Lotus team and won his first Grand Prix. In 1988 Senna joined the McLaren racing team with Alain Prost as his team-mate, marking the beginning of a fierce rivalry between the two. On the track, Senna could be ruthless at times, showing extreme determination and precision. Off the track, Senna was a deeply religious and compassionate man. He created the Senna Foundation, an organization with the aim of helping poor and needy young people in Brazil and the rest of the world. In 1994, he joined the top team at the time, Williams-Renault. In his third race for the team, the San Marino Grand Prix, he went off the track and suffered a fatal crash. His death was considered a national tragedy in Brazil.

◆ see Michael Schumacher p. 210

SHEARER, ALAN (b. 1970)

Not especially tall, or particularly quick come to that, Alan Shearer is a striker who relies on strength and timing. He is also an exceptionally fine header of the ball – probably the best since Andy Gray – and possesses a thumping right foot.

Shearer emerged as a prodigy at Southampton, where he managed to shine in a mediocre side without making the breakthrough at international level. Then Jack Walker's cash, plus the promise of winning the sort of trophies that were always going to elude him at Southampton, lured him to Blackburn Rovers. At Ewood Park Shearer's scoring rate increased immediately, and his prolific partnership with Chris Sutton propelled Blackburn to the league title in 1995. Later he struck up a similarly fruitful partnership for England with Teddy Sheringham, a double-act that climaxed with the destruction of Holland at Wembley in the group stages of Euro 96.

That same year Shearer returned to Newcastle, his boyhood team. Since then he has been hampered by a series of injuries, but when fit has continued to score goals. Now retired from international football to protect his body from further punishment, Shearer has been touted as a managerial successor to Bobby Robson at St James's Park. (*See over for illustration.*)

see David Beckham p. 145

SHILTON, PETER (b. 1949)

Peter Shilton continued playing for so long that it seemed the only thing likely to persuade him to hang up his gloves was the arrival of his bus pass in the post. Having made his debut for Leicester in 1966, aged 17, he was still playing league football aged 47. (*See over for illustration.*)

▶ *OVER: England striker Alan Shearer.*

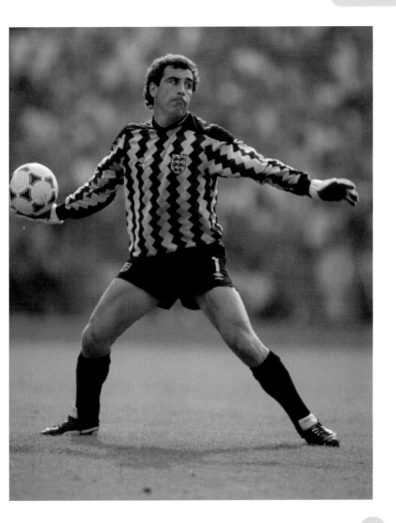

◀ PREVIOUS PAGE: *England goalkeeper Peter Shilton.*

His best spell as a club footballer was in Brian Clough's Nottingham Forest that won the European Cup twice, but he also played in the Southampton side that contained five England captains – himself, Keegan, Watson, Mills and Channon.

For a number of years Shilton played second fiddle or alternated with Ray Clemence in the England goal; at times it seemed that everyone bar the managers could see he was the better of the two men. He later made the number one jersey his own, and though he went on to record a record number of England caps (125), one wonders what tally he may have reached if his international managers had been more decisive. Shilton played in three World Cups, conceding only one goal in the 1982 tournament as England were eliminated without losing. Once he had ironed out early gremlins in his technique, Shilton became the complete goalkeeper. A great shot-stopper, although perhaps not in the same class as Gordon Banks, dominant in the area, and fast off his line.

🔳 *see* David Seaman p. 210

SOBERS, SIR GARFIELD ST AUBRUN (b. 1936)

From the age of 17, when he made his first appearance for the West Indies, Sir Gary was a dazzling batsman, an effective bowler and a brilliant fielder. His versatility with the ball was awesome. During his Test career, he appeared in 93 matches, bettered Sir Len Hutton's record by scoring 365 runs in a single innings, captained his country a record 39 times, made 110 catches and took 235 wickets. Sir Gary was blessed with two vital attributes: he was a great natural athlete, and he was possessed of a wonderful sense of timing. Like many West Indian players, Sir Gary played his club cricket in England, representing Nottinghamshire, and it was

► *OVER: Garfield Sobers for Nottingham playing at Lords versus Middlesex, 14 June 1968.*

whilst playing for them that he compiled one of cricket's most memorable batting records. Playing against Glamorgan at their Swansea ground during the summer of 1968, he faced Malcolm Nash and walloped him for six straight sixes. On the fourth delivery, Sir Gary was actually caught, but the umpire ruled that the fielder's foot had gone over the boundary rope, thereby nullifying the catch. For the record, the shots were over: 1. long-on, 2. long-on, 3. long-off, 4. mid-wicket, 5. long-on, 6. mid-wicket – in short, smashed all over the ground. Fortunately for the world, this game was televised, and as the last ball sailed out of the ground, commentator Peter Walker exclaimed, 'That's not a six. It's a twelve!'

Malcolm Nash, ever the gentleman, took comfort in the fact that he would be immortalized in the pages of Wisden, if not for exactly the right reasons. The last six had been so powerful that the ball had been temporarily lost, only to be found by a small boy several days later, thus fortunately being preserved for posterity. Sir Gary, as ever, remained modest about the whole thing. (*See over for illustration.*)

↕ *see* Don Bradman p. 149

THOMPSON, DALEY (b. 1958)

Daley Thompson is one of the finest athletes Britain has ever produced and one of the best the world has ever seen. The fact that he became famous for winning numerous titles and breaking world records in one of the least glamorous events – the decathlon – demonstrates the extent of his achievements. During the first half of the 1980s, he dominated the event and proved himself the ultimate competitor. Every time it looked like he might lose to any of his arch-rivals, particularly Germany's Jürgen Hingsen, Thompson triumphed again. He thrived in crucial moments,

gaining those vital seconds which made the difference between winning and losing. Thompson was a double Olympic champion, world champion, European champion and Commonwealth champion. Prior to his 1983 triumph at the first World Athletics Championship, he had broken the world record three times and the Commonwealth record nine times. When he won the title in Helsinki in 1983, Thompson became the first athlete ever to hold all four major titles. Allied to his amazing ability and incredible determination to win was an exuberant personality with a ready smile. (*See over for illustration.*)

see Sebastian Coe p. 159

▲ ABOVE: Helsinki, 1983 – Daley Thompson winning the gold for Britain in the World Championship's decathlon javelin event.

VAN BASTEN, MARCO (b. 1964)

If Marco van Basten had not been forced out of the game prematurely, who knows what he might have achieved. He was not yet 30 when a suspect ankle gave way in the 1993 European Cup final, a game in which he probably ought not to have played. That injury meant van Basten was denied the opportunity to make amends for the one failure in his career – a miserable showing in an abject Dutch display at the 1990 World Cup Finals. Van Basten and Bergkamp? Now that would have been interesting.

Still, his admirers – and he had many – can at least console themselves with memories of his performances in Holland's 1988 European Championship success in Germany, where he scored a hat-trick against England, the winner in the semi-final against the hosts, and a sensational volley from an impossible angle in the final against Russia. At club level van Basten won the lot. Starting as a 17-year-old with Ajax, he collected medals galore in Holland before a move to AC Milan in 1987. There, with compatriots Gullit and Rijkaard, he was the spearhead of the best club side in Europe and picked up three Serie A titles and two European Cups. His strike rate against the cynical defences of the Italian league was, to quote David Coleman, quite remarkable.

▣ *see* Johann Cruyff p. 161

WOODS, TIGER (b. 1975)

On 13 April 1997, Tiger Woods did not so much win the US Masters as begin a new era in golf. Quite simply, his victory was so breathtaking, so record-breaking, so complete, that he instantly made himself the biggest name in golf and one of the major sporting superstars in the world. A look through the records he broke shows just how amazing his

▶ *OVER: Marco Van Basten.*

performance was. He went round the famous Augusta course in 270 shots, breaking Jack Nicklaus's and Raymond Floyd's total of 271. His victory margin of 12 shots was the biggest ever recorded since the beginning of championship golf in 1860. His victory, at 21 years old, made him the youngest champion in the 61-year history of the US Masters. During the whole tournament, he played the back nine without bogeying, shooting an incredible 16 under par, thus breaking Arnold Palmer's record, set in 1962, by four shots. Perhaps most significantly for a course and a sport dominated by whites, Woods became the first black player to win a Major championship. To emphasize this, immediately after his victory he became only the third ethnic-minority player to join the Augusta club.

The victory came in Woods' third Masters and was achieved just seven-and-a-half months into his professional career. His victory was assured after the third round, when he shot a seven-under-par 65, to follow his 66 on the second day. After the first round, he was three off the lead. At the end of the second, he was three ahead. By the end of the third round, he was nine shots ahead, before rounding off his victory with a three-under-par 69. His victory was sealed with a par on the final hole. For the last 63 holes, he went round in 22 under par. After his victory, golfing legend Tom Watson said Woods might be a player who 'only comes round in a millennium'. Jack Nicklaus said Woods had ten Masters victories in him. At the heart of his victory was his astonishing power off the tee. His driving averaged 295 m (323.1 yds) throughout the tournament and his putting was superb. His 1997 victory was something the young Californian had been dreaming about his entire short life.

◆ *see* Michael Johnson p. 175

▶ *OVER: Tiger Woods, America's latest golfing sensation and winner of the 1997 US Masters.*

ZICO (b. 1953)

At the 1982 World Cup, inspired by Socrates, Falcão, Cerezo and Zico, Brazil played football of an attacking brilliance not seen since 1970. It was a breath of fresh air after their dour tactics in 1978, and it allowed Zico, a huge disappointment in that earlier tournament, to show his true colours. His wiry strength and fierce shooting added firepower to the intricate movements of the men in gold – which was just as well because their other main striker, Serginho, was a donkey. Brazil's second-phase games were both classics; a 3-1 win over Argentina, featuring three brilliant goals, and an undulating 3-2 defeat by a Paolo Rossi-inspired Italy. Sadly, the 1986 tournament saw Zico back to the fitful and fretful shadow of eight years earlier. Zico's club football was principally with Flamengo, for whom he once starred in a win over a top-notch Liverpool team in the World Club Championship. A £2.5 million move to Udinese proved a bit of a waste of money for the Italians. Indeed, save for that one tournament in 1982, Zico would have been in danger of being remembered as one of the world's great unfulfilled talents.

🔷 *see* Pelé p. 202

◀ *LEFT: Brazilian Zico.*

POLITICS & POWER

ARAFAT, YASSER
(b. 1929)

Chairman of the Palestinian Liberation Organization (PLO) since 1969, Arafat, who always appears in public wearing the symbolic kaffiyeh, presided over the PLO's move from terrorism to diplomacy in the late 1980s. The 1993 Oslo Peace Accord with Israel led to limited Palestinian self-rule in Jericho and the Gaza Strip in 1994, for which Arafat, Shimon Peres and Yitzhak Rabin received the 1994 Nobel Peace Prize. Agreements since then have led to a slow expansion of self-rule in the West Bank and Arafat was elected president of the Palestinian-controlled territory in 1996.

🔲 *see* Mahatma Gandhi p. 244

▲ *ABOVE: Yasser Arafat, Palestinian figurehead and leader of the Palestinian Liberation Organization (PLO).*

BLAIR, TONY (b. 1953)

British prime minister Tony Blair, a former barrister, led the Labour Party to its most comprehensive election victory in May 1997, ending 18 years of Conservative rule. It won 418 seats, the highest ever recorded by Labour, and took its largest share of votes since the 1960s. At 44, Blair was the youngest prime minister since Lord Liverpool in 1812. In power he has maintained a centrist approach which many commentators claim is why Labour were elected in the first place. His style is often described as 'presidential' and he is accused of relying too heavily on 'spin' to get across Labour's political message. A fluent French speaker, Blair has committed British troops to action in Kosovo and Sierra Leone. He has introduced a Scottish Parliament, Welsh Assembly, maintained the peace process in Northern Ireland and partially reformed the House of Lords. Leader of the Labour Party since 1994, Blair is credited with re-inventing the party, re-branding it 'New Labour' and making it more voter attractive. However, his popularity decreased dramatically in 2003 in the controversy surrounding the war in Iraq.

see Margaret Thatcher p. 266

▲ *ABOVE: British Labour prime minister Tony Blair.*

BUSH, GEORGE W. (b. 1946)

George Bush Jnr is the 43rd president of the United States (since 2001). Son of George Bush Snr (41st US president). Bush pipped Democrat Al Gore to the post in one of the most controversial elections in American history, becoming president despite losing the popular vote by 500,000 (out of 105 million cast). Bush was governor of Texas (1995–2000) and a former businessman (he owned an oil company and the Texas Rangers baseball team). His actions, particularly with regards to sending American troops to Iraq in 2003, have seem him villified and lauded in equal measure on the international stage.

🔀 *see* Bill Clinton p. 238

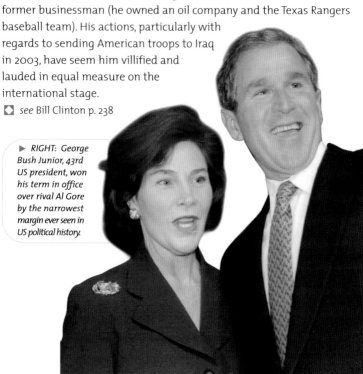

▶ RIGHT: George Bush Junior, 43rd US president, won his term in office over rival Al Gore by the narrowest margin ever seen in US political history.

CAPONE, AL (1899–1947)

The mosy famous American gangster of all time, nicknamed 'Scarface'. Born in Brooklyn, Alphonse Capone received three scars on his face from an insulted girl at school. Capone moved to Chicago (1920) and took over the gangster empire of his uncle during the period of Prohibition. In 1929 he masterminded the St Valentine's Day Massacre, gunning down seven men. Despite his criminal and homicidal activities, no one ever managed to pin the crimes on him and ironically it was for tax evasion that he was eventually caught. He was sentenced to 11 years in Atlanta prison; he was transferred to Alcatraz in 1934, remaining there until 1939. He died in Miami from syphilis.

◆ see Rasputin p. 261

▲ ABOVE: Al Capone, the infamous Chicago gangster, nicknamed 'Scarface'.

CASTRO, FIDEL (b. 1926)

Cuban leader Fidel Castro, together with his brother Raul and Che Guevara, fought a guerilla campaign against the dictator, Batista. On taking power, Castro transformed Cuba into the first Communist state in Latin America, with Marxist reforms of industry and agriculture. He forged close ties with the Soviet Union, and survived political crises with the USA, including the Bay of Pigs invasion and the Cuban missile crisis. A new constitution in 1976 created a National Assembly with Castro as

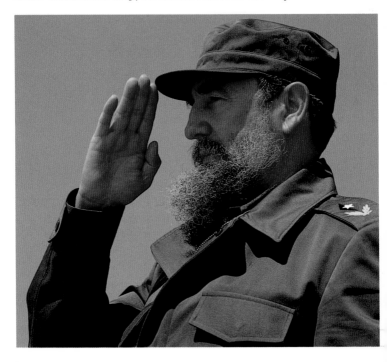

president. The long US economic blockade and the end of large Soviet subsidies have ruined the economy and left Castro isolated. He introduced limited free enterprise following anti-government demonstrations in 1993.

◊ *see* Ernesto 'Che' Guevara p. 247

CEAUCESCU, NICOLAE (1918–89)

Romanian leader Ceaucescu was a member of the Communist youth movement, and was imprisoned in both 1936 and 1940. He escaped from prison in 1944 and served as secretary of the Union of Communist Youth (1944–45), minister of agriculture (1948–50) and deputy minister of the armed forces (1950–54). He succeeded Gheorghiu-Dej as leader in March 1965, head of state (1967) and president of Romania (1974). He was shot by a firing squad, along with his wife, having been convicted of mass murder and other crimes in Timisoara (1989).

◊ *see* Mao Zedong p. 255

CHARLES PHILIP ARTHUR GEORGE, PRINCE OF WALES (b. 1948)

Heir to Queen Elizabeth II and 21st Prince of Wales. On 29 July 1981, he married Lady Diana Spencer. They had two sons, Prince William, born in 1982 and Prince Henry (Harry) born in 1984. The marriage ran into difficulties, and Charles and Diana separated in 1992. They were divorced in 1996. Diana's intense popularity with the British public led to criticism over the way the royal family and Prince Charles in particular treated the princess, and this heightened after her death in 1997. Charles maintained his dignity throughout a difficult time for the monarchy and recent years have seen a revival in his own popularity.

◀ *LEFT: Fidel Castro, Cuba's Communist dictator.*

Prince Charles was born at Buckingham Palace on 14 November 1948, the first of the four children of Elizabeth II (then Princess Elizabeth) and Prince Philip, Duke of Edinburgh. Charles's additional titles are Earl of Chester, Duke of Cornwall, Duke of Rothesay, Earl of Carrick and Baron of Renfrew, Lord of the Isles and Great Steward of Scotland. He was invested Prince of Wales at Caernarvon Castle on 1 July 1969 and as prince, he inherited the Duchy of Cornwall, reserved for the heir to the throne. In 1971, at Cambridge University, Charles became the first heir to the British Crown to earn a master's degree, and afterwards served in the Royal Navy (1971–76). Charles founded the Prince's Trust, a charitable organization, while in the Navy. Prince Charles has been an outspoken critic of modern architecture and is a champion of organic farming.

see Diana, Princess of Wales p. 240

CHAMBERLAIN, NEVILLE (1869–1940)

Chamberlain had been involved in politics since the early 1900s. In the aftermath of World War I he held a number of senior political posts including minister of health (1924–29) and chancellor of the Exchequer (1931–37). When Chamberlain came to power as prime minister (1937), he agreed that the Germans had legitimate grievances arising out of the settlement after World War I. His policies, which became known as 'appeasement', allowed the Anschluss, the union of Germany and Austria in 1938, which had been forbidden by Treaty of Versailles. When Hitler demanded control of German-speaking Czechoslovakia (Sudetenland), Chamberlain signed the Munich Agreement, on 29 September 1938. With this, it seemed that war had been avoided, but in March 1939 Hitler seized the rest of Czechoslovakia and Chamberlain realized that Hitler could not be trusted. When German troops rolled across the Polish border in September 1939, Chamberlain was forced to declare war. He proved to be an inept war leader in the ensuing months and he was eventually replaced by Winston Churchill.

◆ *see* Winston Churchill p. 237

CHURCHILL, WINSTON (1874–1965)

Following a successful – if controversial – British army career, Churchill became a war correspondent in 1899. He was elected as an MP the following year and subsequently served in numerous positions between 1906 and 1915; he chose to rejoin the army and served on the Western Front during World War I. Churchill returned to politics after the war, by 1933 his extreme views on rearmament and his opposition to Hitler's Germany caused his fall from favour. Despite uncertainty about his methods and beliefs, Chamberlain appointed Churchill First Lord of the Admiralty in April 1940;

▶ RIGHT: Winston Churchill, one of Britain's most influential statesmen.

a month later Chamberlain resigned and Churchill was asked to form a government.

Churchill developed a strong relationship with the Unites States, leading to the Lend-Lease Agreement (March 1941), his leadership keeping Britain afloat in the early war years. After the attack on Pearl Harbor in December 1941, Churchill worked with US president Franklin D. Roosevelt to ensure victory over the Axis Powers, welcoming Russia on board to develop a united strategy. Churchill resisted the opening of a European front in 1943 despite Russian pressure and the collapse of Germany and Italy in North Africa. With victory at hand two years later, Churchill lost power in a landslide Labour victory, but returned in 1951. He retired from public life in 1955 due to ill-health and died on 24 January 1965.

◘ *see* Neville Chamberlain p. 236

CLINTON, BILL (b. 1946)

Bill Clinton was president of the US between 1993 and 2001. First elected Arkansas governor in 1976, he defeated George Bush in 1993. Clinton's battles with a Republican-dominated Congress meant he was unable to pass healthcare reforms, although he did increase the minimum wage. Foreign policy successes included restoring relations with Vietnam and a role as peacemaker in Bosnia and Northern Ireland. But his presidency was dogged by scandal, including the Whitewater Case and his affair with Monica Lewinsky. Clinton was the first sitting president to testify before a grand jury and he narrowly avoided impeachment after committing perjury. His wife, Hillary Rodham Clinton, is Senator of New York.

◘ *see* George W. Bush p. 232

▶ *RIGHT: Former US president Bill Clinton.*

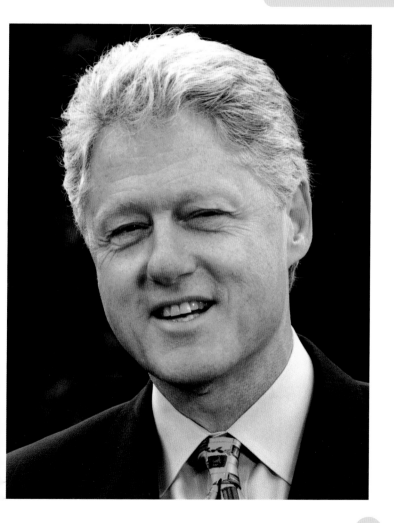

DE GAULLE, CHARLES (1890–1970)

French general and statesman Charles De Gaulle was an army officer in World War I and, while in exile, head of the French Resistance during World War II. A chequered political career followed, including stints as president and provisional head of state. De Gaulle became president (with a new constitution that strengthened the role) in 1958. He was determined to resolve the crisis created by the civil war in Algeria (a French colony) and in 1962, he negotiated Algeria's independence. De Gaulle's high spending on nuclear defence, among other things, sparked demonstrations by workers and students in 1968 that nearly brought down his government. He resigned the following year.

see Winston Churchill p. 237

▲ *ABOVE: Charles de Gaulle on the cover of* Time *magazine. De Gaulle became leader of the French troops during the German occupation of France. He was head of the provisional French government from 1944–46.*

DIANA, PRINCESS OF WALES (1961–97)

Diana, daughter of Earl Spencer, married Prince Charles on 29 July 1981. She achieved phenomenal worldwide popularity as a fashion icon, for her charitable work and as devoted mother to her two sons, William and Harry. Diana became the most photographed woman in the world and attracted intense media interest. The marriage dissolved due to allegations that Charles was having an affair; Diana is also believed to have had an affair. In 1992, she contributed to a book *Diana, Her True Story* by Andrew Morton, which revealed the truth about her so-called 'fairytale' marriage. The book created a scandal and Diana and Charles separated the same year. They divorced four years later. Diana continued her charity work and, among other projects, championed a campaign against anti-personnel mines

organized by the Red Cross organization. In 1997, Diana was in Paris with her friend Dodi Fayed when their car crashed while being pursued by paparazzi. Dodi was killed and Diana, who was severely injured, died a few hours later. Her funeral in London attracted extraordinary public grief. Diana was afterwards buried at the Spencer family home, Althorp House, in Northamptonshire.

◆ *see* Prince Charles p. 235

▲ *ABOVE: Britain's 'Queen of Hearts', Diana, Princess of Wales.*

EISENHOWER, DWIGHT D. (1890–1969)

Prior to 1942, Eisenhower's military career had been less than impressive, yet in March of that year he was sent to Britain as leader of the European Theatre of Operations. Eisenhower was given command of Operation Torch (8 November 1942), the Allied landings in north-west Africa. Supporting Montgomery's 8th Army, advancing from Egypt, Axis resistance was defeated by May 1943.

Eisenhower, now a full General, began organizing the invasion of Italy, beginning with Sicily (July 1943) then the mainland (September 1943). He was given the responsibility of organizing three million troops for the full invasion of Europe as Head of Supreme Headquarters Allied Expeditionary Force (SHAEF). Eisenhower continued in this role until the fall of Germany in 1945.

Eisenhower retired in 1948, but became supreme commander of NATO in 1951 and on 20 January 1953 became president of the United States. He oversaw the Korean War (1950–53) and was re-elected in 1956. When he finally left office, he concentrated on writing his memoirs, published between 1963 and 1967. Eisenhower, possibly one of the most popular US presidents of all time, and the first soldier to become president since Ulysses S. Grant in 1869. He died at Gettysburg on 28 March 1969.

◆ see Winston Churchill p. 237

ELIZABETH II (b. 1926)

The daughter of George VI, Elizabeth became heir presumptive to the throne after her uncle, Edward VIII, abdicated in 1936. She succeeded the throne after the untimely death of her father in 1952. The half-century in which she has ruled has been one of enormous change for the monarchy, but Elizabeth has remained a dutiful and well-informed queen.

As young girls, Elizabeth and her younger sister Margaret became known as 'The Little Princesses' and they were the darlings of the press and the public. Their relationship with their parents was very loving. Their mother, Queen Elizabeth, later Queen Mother, brought them up to be aware of their royal responsibilities. King George was passionately attached to Elizabeth. It was George who talked of 'Us Four' – the close family unit comprising himself, his wife, Elizabeth and Margaret.

Elizabeth married Lieutenant Philip Mountbatten RN, a distant cousin, in 1947. He became Prince Philip, Duke of Edinburgh. They subsequently had four children. Elizabeth and Philip built up a strong family based image with their four children, but this was badly dented by the scandals later surrounding their heir, Prince Charles, and his wife Diana.

As princess, she publicly dedicated herself to the service of her people. As queen, Elizabeth has proved a non-controversial monarch with a strong sense of duty. She has made frequent state visits overseas and takes part in regular royal ceremonials at home, including most importantly the State Opening of Parliament and the ceremony at the Cenotaph at Whitehall, London, commemorating Britain's war dead. Elizabeth is head of the Commonwealth, which is made up of former territories of the British Empire. In private life, the Queen is an expert on horses.

↔ see Prince Charles p. 235

▶ RIGHT: Queen Elizabeth II.

FERDINAND, FRANZ (1863–1914)

Heir to the Habsburg crowns of Austria and Hungary, through his uncle, Emperor Franz Josef I, Franz Ferdinand was highly committed to the monarchy. He acted against the nobility who challenged imperial authority, but he was also prepared to consider reform. He was profoundly opposed to Serbian nationalism and visited Sarajevo in Bosnia on 28 June 1914. He and his wife were assassinated there by Serbian nationalists, 'The Black Hand', triggering events leading to the outbreak of World War I.

◆ *see* Neville Chamberlain p. 236

FRANCO, FRANCISCO (1892–1975)

As army general, Franco led the Nationalist rebels to victory in the Spanish Civil War (1936–39). With help from a fascist Italy and Nazi Germany, Franco invaded Spain from Morocco and established a corporate state of which he was dictator. He kept Spain officially out of World War II, although he sent aid to the German side, and in 1947 he declared Spain a kingdom and himself regent. In 1969 he named Prince Juan Carlos as his successor.

◆ *see* Benito Mussolini p. 256

GANDHI, MAHATMA (1869–1948)

Pacifist Indian nationalist leader Mohandas Gandhi was given the name Mahatma, meaning 'great sage'. Trained as a barrister in Britain, Gandhi practised in South Africa until he led the Indian

▶ *RIGHT: Mahatma Gandhi, the Indian nationalist and spiritual leader.*

community against discrimination in 1914. Gandhi then returned to India where he gained influence in the Congress Party and led a programme of non-cooperation in pursuit of Indian independence. His campaign was dedicated to non-violence, religious toleration and the ending of caste discrimination, but he was frequently imprisoned. Gandhi was assassinated by a Hindu fanatic in the violence which followed independence in 1947.

see Martin Luther King p. 277

GOERING, HERMANN (1893–1946)

An air ace with 22 kills to his name, Goering had been awarded the Iron Cross during World War I. He was recruited into the Nazi Party in 1922, and was involved in the Munich Beer Hall Putsch of 1923. Goering fled Germany after the coup, returning in 1927 and working to bring the Nazis to power. Goering was made Commander-in-Chief of the Luftwaffe in 1935 and directed campaigns against Poland (1939) and France (1940).

The Luftwaffe began their air assault on Britain in August 1940, as a prelude to the planned invasion. They failed, however, and Hitler never forgave Goering. From 1943 the Luftwaffe came under increasing pressure, reduced as it was to defensive operations against the growing air power of the Allies. Goering sank into depression, undermined by others now closer to Hitler, who decreed he would remain in Berlin until the end. Goering mistook this as a signal to seize the reins of power in Germany, but instead was dismissed from his posts, expelled from the Nazi Party and subsequently arrested. Captured by US troops in May 1945, Goering was a key figure at the Nuremberg trials. He was found guilty on four counts of war crimes and sentenced to death by hanging.

On 5 October 1946, two hours before his scheduled execution, he committed suicide in his cell.

see Adolf Hitler p. 248

GORBACHEV, MIKHAIL
(b. 1931)

The last president of the USSR (1988–91), Gorbachev's policies of *glasnost* ('openness') and *perestroika* ('restructuring') radically altered Soviet society. They also led ultimately the break-up of the USSR and downfall of Communism in Eastern Europe. In 1991 hard-liners attempted to overthrow Gorbachev, and by the end of the year he resigned as president, following the formation of the Commonwealth of Independent States led by Boris Yeltsin which had left him out of a job.

◆ see Boris Yeltsin p. 268

▶ RIGHT: Mikhail Gorbachev, former president of the Soviet Union, is best remembered today for his policies of *perestroika* and *glasnost* which were partly responsible for bringing an end to Communism in Russia.

▼ BELOW: Che Guevara, Cuban revolutionary and writer, joined forces with the Castro brothers in the 1960s and formed a guerilla movement to depose Batista.

GUEVARA, ERNESTO 'CHE' (1928–67)

Cuban revolutionary. Argentine-born doctor and political activist, Ernesto 'Che' Guevara joined Cuban brothers Fidel and Raul Castro in their guerilla campaign to overthrow Fulgencio Batista. He was Castro's chief lieutenant in the revolution (1956–59) and served as minister of industry (1961–65) in the

new government. He left Cuba to train revolutionaries in Africa and Latin America, but was caught and executed by the Bolivian army in 1967.

◆ see Fidel Castro p. 234

HITLER, ADOLF (1889–1945)

Hitler was born in Austria, spending his early years in poverty in Vienna and Munich. In his mid twenties he served in World War I as a volunteer and began developing fascist ideas to satisfy his anger at the treatment

of Germany after the war. By 1921 he was leader of the National Socialist German Workers Party, which he abbreviated to 'Nazi Party'. Hitler used the Nazi Party as his vehicle for nurturing hatred toward races and creeds that he blamed for the humiliating plight of the German people. By 1933 he had become chancellor of a Nazi–Nationalist coalition. 1934 saw the suppression of the Nationalist contingent and Hitler became Führer. Hitler led the Anschluss with Austria in 1938 and whipped Germany into a frenzy of nationalism in the preparation for World War II. Throughout the war he remained the driving force behind the German campaign, but committed suicide when he realized that the Central Powers were facing defeat.

◘ *see* Hermann Goering p. 245

HO CHI MINH (1890–1969)

President of North Vietnam (1954–69). Minh was the leader of the Vietnamese nationalist movement for nearly three decades. After spending time in Moscow, he returned to Vietnam in World War II to found the Communist Viet Minh (1941), the Vietnamese independence movement. His army fought the Japanese when they invaded the country, and drove out the French colonial regime in the Indochina War (1946–54). The Geneva conference in 1954 divided Vietnam in half, and Minh became the first president of North Vietnam. Peace did not last and he lived to see the start of war against the US-backed government of South Vietnam.

◘ *see* Pol Pot p. 259

◀ *LEFT: Adolf Hitler, surrounded by his henchmen, delivers the nefarious Nazi Party salute to the crowds.*

HUSSEIN, SADDAM (b. 1937)

Saddam Hussein came to power in 1968. He suppressed opposition with great violence, spreading deep terror across all classes of Iraqi society. Saddam became president of Iraq in 1979 and in 1980 embarked on a damaging war with neighbouring Iran, where a new, Islamic fundamentalist government had just come to power. The war, which caused great loss of life on both sides, ended in 1988, the year Saddam mounted a ferocious persecution of the Kurds in northern Iraq. In 1990 Hussein invaded Kuwait. This resulted in the Gulf War, in which the Iraqis were attacked by a coalition force, led by the US. Saddam lost the war, but remained president of Iraq. Subsequently, the UN attempted to force him to relinquish the weapons of mass destruction he was thought to possess. In 2003, a second war took place and Saddam's regime, which was also suspected of aiding terrorists, was destroyed and the leader captured.

see George W. Bush p. 232

▶ *RIGHT: Saddam Hussein.*

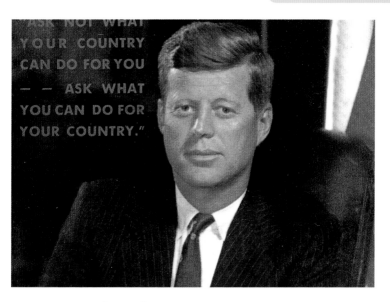

KENNEDY, JOHN F. (1917–63)

John F. Kennedy was the 35th US president, serving between 1961 and 1963. At 43 Kennedy was the youngest-ever president. Many of his domestic reforms, such as civil rights and extra spending on education and welfare, stalled in Congress. His time was spent dealing with foreign affairs, including the Bay of Pigs invasion, the Cuban missile crisis (1962) – the peaceful outcome of which was a personal triumph for Kennedy, and increasing the number of US military advisers to South Vietnam to 16,000 (1963). Kennedy was assassinated while campaigning for a second term.

◆ see Bill Clinton p. 238

▲ ABOVE: John F. Kennedy.

KHRUSHCHEV, NIKITA (1894–1971)

Russian premier Nikita Krushchev rose rapidly in the Communist Party, directing the second five-year plan and the Red Army's southern front during World War II. He became the Soviet agricultural expert when he was charged with restoring agricultural production after the war. After Stalin's death Krushchev was appointed head of the Communist Party, but he denounced Stalin and demoted many of his supporters. He was made Soviet premier on the resignation of Bulganin in 1958, until he himself was deposed in 1964 following accusations of political error over the Cuban missile crisis. He was dropped from the party in 1966.

◼ see Mikhail Gorbachev p. 246

LENIN, VLADIMIR ILYICH (1870–1924)

The Russian revolutionary and political theoretician Vladimir Ilyich Lenin created the Soviet Union and headed its first government (1917–24). After the failure of the 1905 revolution, he spent time in exile where he wrote many revolutionary pamphlets, including *State and Revolution*, his most important contribution to Marxist political theory. Lenin adapted Marxism to Russian conditions to create Leninism. In 1917 the Bolsheviks came to power and Lenin was finally able to put his theories into practice, although civil war broke out between 1918–21. After the war Lenin introduced the New Economic Policy, which returned the Soviet Union to a market economy, at the same time insisting on single-party rule. (*See over for illustration.*)

◼ see Joseph Stalin p. 263

◀ *LEFT: Russian premier Nikita Khrushchev.*

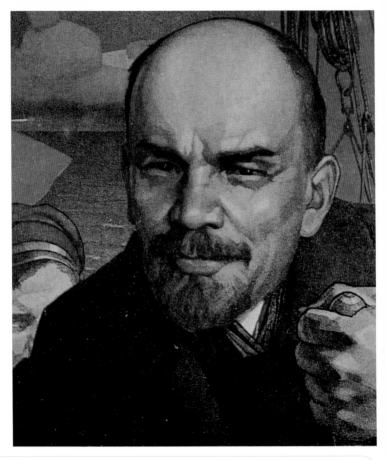

▲ ABOVE: *Vladimir Lenin changed the face of Imperial Russia by ensuring all businesses became property of the State.*

LLOYD GEORGE, DAVID (1863–1945)

David Lloyd George first entered politics as a Liberal in 1890 and subsequently held several important ministerial posts in British governments. A spellbinding orator, he passionately promoted the cause of social reform and improvement in the lives of ordinary working people. Among his greatest political achievements were the Old Age Pensions Act (1908) and the 'People's Budget' (1909–10). In 1921, Lloyd George's power-base fractured after a serious split occurred within the Liberal Party. The Liberals lost the general election of 1922 and never won power again. Lloyd George remained an MP until his death in 1945.

◳ *see* Winston Churchill p. 237

MAO ZEDONG (1893–1976)

Mao Zedong was the founder of the People's Republic of China and Chinese leader (1949–76). He has been described as the 'architect of the new China'. A founding member of the Chinese Communist Party in 1921, he became a dedicated Communist and expert soldier. After heading the famous Long March in 1934–35 (a 9,700-km/15,520-mile trek) Mao became the Communist Party leader.

In 1949 Mao became the Communist Party Chairman and declared the People's Republic of China. Under Mao's radical reforms all land was distributed to the peasants, farms run communally and industry controlled by the State.

Two of Mao's national campaigns, 'The Great Leap Forward' (1958) and the 'Cultural Revolution' (1966), failed in advancing China. They led to the collapse of the economy and the execution of millions – and widespread unrest resulted.

◳ *see* Joseph Stalin p. 263

MONTGOMERY, BERNARD (1887–1976)

Montgomery began his military career in 1908, serving in India and on the Western Front during World War I. He remained in the army during the interwar years, reaching the rank of Major-General by 1938. In June 1940, he extricated his 2nd Corps out of France via Dunkirk and was given several UK-based commands until July 1942. Montgomery was then offered command of the 8th Army in Egypt to face Rommel.

On 23 October 1942 he launched Operation Lightfoot, which failed to meet its objectives; on 1 November, however, his Operation Supercharge broke through the German and Italian lines, recapturing Tobruk and Tripoli, and forcing the Axis surrender in North Africa. Montgomery was instrumental in the invasion of Sicily and the Italian mainland (July–October 1943), and in command of all ground troops for D-Day (Operation Overlord) in June 1944. He also masterminded Operation Market Garden in September 1944.

In 1945 Montgomery became Commander of the British occupation troops in Germany and later Deputy Supreme Commander of Allied forces in Europe, under General Eisenhower. The great general died on 25 March 1976.

◆ *see* Erwin Rommel p. 262

MUSSOLINI, BENITO (1883–1945)

Mussolini was the leader (Il Duce) of Italian Fascism, which he founded in 1919. His Blackshirt militia, supported by landowners and industrialists, terrorized socialist and peasant groups. He formed a coalition government in 1922 and by 1926 had created a totalitarian, single-party state. Mussolini invaded Ethiopia (1935–36), but the Italian army suffered many defeats in World War II, which they entered in 1940 in support of Germany. Mussolini was forced to resign from the Fascist Council in 1943. With

LA TRIBUNA ILLUSTRATA

Supplemento illustrato de "La Tribuna"

Anno XLV - N 40   3 ottobre 1937 - Anno XV   Cent. 40 il numero

LA STORICA VISITA DEL DUCE AL FÜHRER
I due Condottieri acclamati dal grande popolo tedesco

▲ ABOVE: Benito Mussolini, leader of the Fascist Party in Italy, became Aldolf Hitler's principal ally during World War II.

German help he set up a republican government in northern Italy, but was captured in 1945 and executed by the partisans.

◆ *see* Adolf Hitler p. 248

NICHOLAS II OF RUSSIA (1868–1918)

Nicholas's rule saw Russia ravaged by World War I and society turned upside down by communist revolutions. A kind and gentle man, close to his family, Nicholas II was happily married to the Tsarina Alexandra who bore him four daughters and one son. The Tsar rejected liberal movements in Russia and supported the suppression of any suggestion of socialist revolution or reform. He preferred the support of old-fashioned conservative advisers and politicians.

Russia was defeated by Japan in the war of 1904–05, a humiliation which led to the formation of a parliament (duma), but it was soon rendered impotent. The outbreak of the war allowed these problems to be shelved but setbacks and government mismanagement exposed them once more, particularly when Nicholas himself took control of the Russian armies, leading to major mistakes in the campaign and causing the Revolution in 1917. Nicholas was forced to abdicate, and the family were imprisoned and executed in July 1918.

◆ *see* Rasputin p. 261

NIXON, RICHARD (1913–94)

Richard Nixon was the 37th US president (1969–74). Under threat of impeachment over the Watergate scandal, Nixon became the first American president to resign from office. He was vice-president to Eisenhower (1953–61) but lost the presidential election to John F. Kennedy in 1960. He won in 1968 and again in 1972. The Nixon Doctrine called for the US withdrawal from Vietnam and he forged new links with China. Nixon's time in office was cut short by the Watergate scandal, which uncovered many dirty tricks by the Republicans: burglary and wiretapping the Democrats' headquarters (at the Watergate offices); a 'slush fund' for discrediting his political opponents during Nixon's re-election campaign; and the subsequent cover-up operation authorized by the president. The existence of the Watergate tapes (Nixon's taped phone conversations) and his reluctance to release them untampered to the investigating committee led to a likely impeachment. Nixon resigned but was later pardoned by his successor, Gerald Ford.

see Bill Clinton p. 238

Pol Pot (c. 1925–1998)

Cambodian politician and revolutionary leader. In 1975, the Cambodian government was toppled by the Khmer Rouge communist rebellion. Pol Pot's leadership of the new 'Democratic Kampuchea' plunged Cambodia into an orgy of civilian massacres until a Vietnamese invasion officially ended his rule in 1979. In 1997 Pol Pot was tried and imprisoned.

see Ho Chi Minh p. 249

▲ ABOVE: The Museum of Genocide in Cambodia displays skulls and other human remains as a gruesome reminder of Pol Pot's atrocities.

PU YI (1906–67)

Pu Yi was the last emperor of China, of the Ch'ing dynasty. Henry Pu Yi, or P'u-i, succeeded as emperor with the name Hsuan Tung in 1908. He was deposed in 1912, ending two millennia of imperial rule (267 years by the Ch'ing). He was briefly restored in 1917, but throughout continued to live in the palace at Beijing. During the Japanese occupation of Manchuria from 1931–45 he was installed as their puppet emperor of Manchukuo. After World War II he was imprisoned as a war criminal from 1950. Released in 1959, he then worked in a botanical garden.

◆ see Mao Zedong p. 255

▶ *RIGHT: Pu Yi, the last emperor of China, became a puppet king in the hands of the Japanese.*

RASPUTIN (1872–1916)

Rasputin was a mysterious Russian figure associated with the court of Tsar Nicholas II. Rasputin was reputed to be a saint, a mystic and a healer. He achieved fame after apparently healing the Tsar's son who was a haemophiliac. Rasputin became great friends with the Tsarina and was said to exert influence over the Tsar's political decisions. Several attempts were made on his life, but he survived them all, including poisoning and being shot. He was finally killed only when he was thrown into the Neva River.

◆ see Nicholas II of Russia p. 258

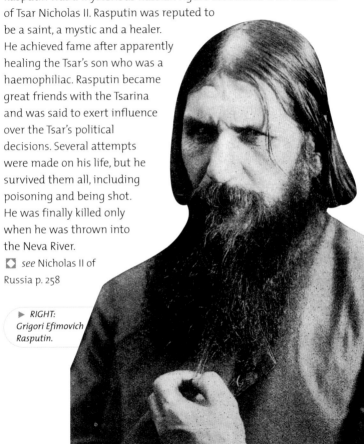

▶ RIGHT:
Grigori Efimovich Rasputin.

ROMMEL, ERWIN (1891–1944)

Rommel, a career soldier, joined the German army in 1910, receiving the Iron Cross for bravery during World War I and remaining in the small interwar German army. In 1939 he was promoted to Major-General and served in Poland. Commanding 7th Panzer Division from February 1940, he planned the campaign against the western nations, launching the invasion and reaching Cherbourg on 19 June 1940.

In February 1941, he commanded the Deutsches Afrika Korps in Tripoli and swept across North Africa on the offensive. Despite setbacks he was only 240 km (150 miles) from Cairo by the end of June 1942. At El Alamein he could make no further headway. The Allies launched their offensive in October, and pursued the 'Desert Fox' back across North Africa. He relinquished command in March, two months before the German surrender in North Africa.

Transferred to France in December 1943, to assist in the defence of Europe, Rommel was injured in an aircraft attack on 17 July 1944. Three days later – implicated in the plot to assassinate Hitler – he was given the choice of suicide or execution as a traitor; he chose suicide. Rommel was undoubtedly the most feared and respected of all German commanders.

◧ *see* Bernard Montgomery p. 256

ROOSEVELT, FRANKLIN D. (1882–1945)

Roosevelt was born in New York and attended Harvard University and Colombia Law School; he married in 1905. His heart was set on a career in politics and he was elected to the New York Senate in 1910. President Woodrow Wilson appointed him assistant secretary of the navy. He was nominated for vice president in 1920 but in the summer of 1921 he was struck with an illness – probably polio – which temporarily cost him the use of his legs, but he was sufficiently recovered to attend the 1924 Democratic convention. In 1928 he became governor of New York. Roosevelt became president in November 1932, serving the first of four terms. The US was in the middle of the Depression at the time, with 13 million people unemployed. In the first few days of his presidency, Roosevelt enacted a sweeping recovery programme which turned the country around. He adopted an isolationist policy but was firmly and implacably opposed to the Nazi regime and the intentions of Japan. He was a reluctant partner militarily but not materially prior to the attack on Pearl Harbor, but after this he mobilized the United States into an irresistible fighting machine. Roosevelt died before he could see the fruits of his victories, on 12 April 1945.

◆ *see* Winston Churchill p. 237

SELASSIE, HAILE (d. 1975)

Emperor of Ethiopia from 1930, Haile Selassie is regarded as the 225th descendant in a line of succession traced back to King Solomon. He took the titles King of Kings, Lord of Lords, and Conquering Lion of the Tribes of Judah. Although now dead, Rastafarians believe his presence can still be felt as Jah (God).

◆ *see* Pu Yi p. 260

STALIN, JOSEPH (1879–1953)

In 1929, Stalin introduced the first Five-Year Plan which enforced the government control of agriculture. Farmers resisted by destroying stock and crops: a huge famine resulted and millions of peasants were detained in Siberian labour camps. During the 1930s 'Great Purge', secret police arrested citizens suspected of challenging the government, and millions were killed. In World War II Stalin aligned

◀ LEFT: Soviet leader, Joseph Stalin.

the USSR with the Allies, and was one of the three world leaders at the 1945 Yalta Conference. In the postwar period Stalin succeeded in isolating the USSR from the West during a period known as the Cold War.

◆ see Adolf Hitler p. 248

▲ ABOVE: Churchill, Roosevelt and Stalin at the Yalta Conference in 1945.

THATCHER, MARGARET (b. 1925)

Thatcher was the longest-serving prime minister in twentieth-century Britain and the first woman to ever hold the post. Nicknamed the 'Iron Lady', her policies were characterized by her firm approach to domestic issues and her militaristic stance in foreign affairs. She advocated privatization and the free market, but was sceptical about Britain's participation in the European Economic Community.

Promoting an agenda of 'sound money' policies, she launched her privatization programme (selling off state-owned enterprises to the private sector) at a time when unemployment, inflation and interest rates all rose. These unpopular policies were offset by Thatcher's great

triumph during her first term: the British victory in the 1982 Falklands War. Internationally, Thatcher opposed unilateral nuclear disarmament and sanctions against South Africa. She was, however, the first Western leader to meet with the new Soviet leader, Mikhail Gorbachev. Following resistance to her leadership style within her party, Thatcher resigned in 1990.

◆ *see* Tony Blair p. 231

▲ *ABOVE: Former British prime minister, Margaret Thatcher.*

TROTSKY, LEON
(1879–1940)

Leon Trotsky is the adopted name of Lev Davidovich Bronstein, Russian revolutionary and Communist theorist. Trotsky was one of the leaders in Russia's October Revolution (1917) and in the civil war that followed (1918–20). After Lenin's death (1924), Trotsky lost the battle for power to Joseph Stalin and was exiled to Mexico.

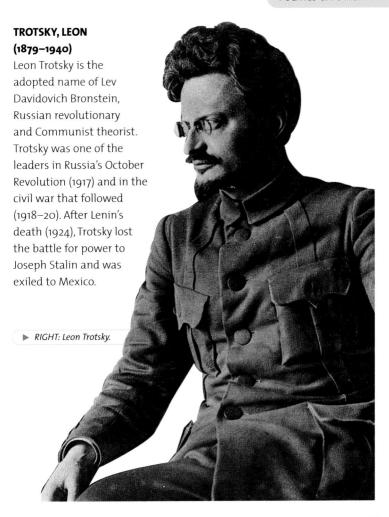

▶ RIGHT: Leon Trotsky.

267

He continued to oppose Stalin and criticized the Soviet regime in his writing until his assassination by an ice pick, probably carried out at Stalin's instigation.

see Joseph Stalin p. 263

WILLIAM, PRINCE (b. 1982)

William is the elder son of Charles, Prince of Wales. Second heir to the throne after his father. Prince William made his first official public appearance when he accompanied his parents on their tour of Australia in 1983. Despite intense public interest, the media granted Prince William an unusual degree of privacy, for a member of the royal family, during his schooldays. During his 'gap' year before university, William travelled on adventure expeditions to South America and Africa.

He is currently studing at St Andrews University in Scotland, where he attempts to live as ordinary a life as possible; however, as the prince grows older, the privacy the media have previously granted him seems to be slipping away, and recent photographs of him with female friends have hit the headlines.

see Prince Charles p. 235, Diana, Princess of Wales p. 240

YELTSIN, BORIS (b. 1931)

An outspoken critic of the traditional Soviet structure, Yeltsin was elected president of Russia in 1991. He was a key figure in the break-up of the Soviet Union and moved Russia towards a market economy. In 1993 he instated both a new parliament and constitution. Despite ill-health and growing unpopularity due to the long war in Chechnya, Yeltsin was re-elected in 1996. He resigned in 2000, naming Vladimir Putin as his successor.

see Mikhail Gorbachev p. 246

▲ ABOVE: Prince William, second in line to the throne after Prince Charles.

HUMAN RIGHTS, SOCIETY & RELIGION

BADEN-POWELL, ROBERT (1857–1941)

After serving the British army with quiet distinction in India and Afghanistan, Baden-Powell became a public figure in the Boer War of 1899–1900 when he won fame as hero of the Siege of Mafeking. In 1908 his book, *Scouting for Boys,* became the basis of a worldwide movement of Boy Scouts. With his help, his sister Agnes founded the Girl Guides two years later, while a movement for younger boys, the Wolf Cubs, followed in 1916.

see Winston Churchill p. 237

BIKO, STEPHEN (1946–77)

Stephen Biko was the founder of South Africa's Black Consciousness Movement. In 1968 he became the first president of the South African Students' Organization, aiming to increase black self-esteem and consciousness, spreading into communities throughout South Africa (1970s). Biko was considered a danger to the apartheid government and was repeatedly arrested. His death in custody in 1977 caused an outcry.

see Nelson Mandela p. 279

DALAI LAMA (b. 1935)

The Tibetan religious leader was born Lhamo Thondup at Takstera in Northern Tibet, Tenzin Gyatso was identified as the 14th Dalai Lama when he was four years old. He assumed temporal power when he was 15 but had to flee Tibet after the Chinese invasion of 1959. He has lived in the West since then. The Gelig (Geluk) School of Buddhism in Tibet developed a line of Dalai Lamas (almost Buddhist saints). He has written 40 books teaching a message of love, compassion and non-violence. He was awarded the Nobel Peace Prize in 1989. He is referred to as 'Gyalwa Rinpoche' by Tibetans ('Precious Eminence').

see Pu Yi p. 260

▲ ABOVE: His Holiness the 14th Dalai Lama fled Tibet after the invasion of the Chinese in 1959.

ESQUIVEL, ADOLFO PEREZ (b. 1931)

Esquival is the Argentinian leader of the Servicio de Paz y Justicia (Peace and Justice Service), a Christian human rights group. A sculptor and architect by profession, he was awarded the Nobel Peace Prize in 1980.

◆ see Dalai Lama p. 272

FREUD, SIGMUND (1856–1939)

In 1873 the Austrian psychologist Sigmund Freud graduated from Sperl Gymnasium and joined the University of Vienna. In 1882 he trained with the psychiatrist Theodor Meynert and Hermann Nothnagel at the General Hospital in Vienna and was appointed lecturer in neuropathology in 1885. Freud opened a clinical practice in neuropsychology in Vienna and continued this work for almost 50 years, studying hysteria, psychological disorders, human bisexuality, erotogenic zones, free association, resistance and unconscious thoughts. In 1895 he wrote *Project for a Scientific Psychology* (published in 1950, 11 years after his death). Freud has been called 'the most influential intellectual legislator of his age'.

◆ see Carl Jung p. 276

◀ LEFT: Sigmund Freud, father of psychoanalysis.

▼ *BELOW: Pope John Paul II resides at the Vatican in Rome.*

JOHN PAUL II (b. 1920)

Born in Wadowice, near Krakow, Poland, Karol Wojtyela moved to Krakow when he was 18 and studied Polish language and literature at university. During World War II he worked in a factory and in 1946 was ordained, gaining a doctorate at Rome in 1948. He continued to lecture at universities in Poland before becoming a bishop in 1958 and Archbishop of Krakow in 1963. After becoming a cardinal in 1967, he was elected pope in 1978. He travelled extensively throughout the world, the first non-Italian pope for centuries, surviving an assassination attempt in 1981. He has been keen to re-establish and re-affirm traditional Catholic values on social, political and theological matters.

see Desmond Tutu p. 275

JUNG, CARL (1875–1961)

Forming an alternative school to that of Sigmund Freud, the Swiss psychologist and psychiatrist Carl Jung had studied at the University of Basel and in Paris. He worked at the University of Zurich as a physician and lecturer from 1900–13, becoming Professor of Psychology at Federal Polytechnical University of Zurich (1933–41) and University of Basel (1943). He developed the theories of introverts, extroverts and the unconscious mind, and wrote *Modern Man in Search of a Soul* (1933) and *Memories, Dreams, Reflections (1962)*.

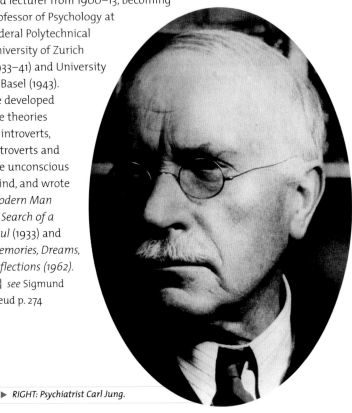

◆ *see* Sigmund Freud p. 274

▶ *RIGHT: Psychiatrist Carl Jung.*

KING, MARTIN LUTHER (1929–68)

Son of an Ebenezer, a Baptist Church pastor, King was ordained in 1947, became pastor of the Dexter Avenue Baptist Church in Montgomery (1954) and received a PhD in theology (1955) as well as heading the Montgomery Improvement Association, formed to boycott the segregation of the city's buses. In 1957 he was awarded the Spingarn Medal by the National Association for the Advancement of Colored People and was voted President of the Southern Christian Leadership Conference in 1958. He visited India the following year to study Gandhi's non-violent protest techniques, holding a non-violent protest against discrimination in 1961. He was arrested in 1963 during campaigns for desegregation in Alabama, received the Nobel Peace Prize in 1964, being the youngest ever recipient, regarding it as a tribute for the Civil Rights movement. Making a stand against the Vietnam War, believing money could have been used to combat poverty and condemning the violence of war, he planned the Poor People's Campaign, marching on Washington (1968). His influence led to the Civil Rights Act (1964) and the Voting Rights Act (1965). He was assassinated in 1968.

◑ *see* Malcolm X p. 277

MALCOLM X (1925–65)

The black American militant leader Malcolm X was born Malcolm Little. Whilst imprisoned in 1946 he was converted to the Black Muslim faith and on his release in 1952 changed his name. He became an effective speaker for the Nation of Islam and founded 'Muhammad Speaks' (1961). He rejected integration and racial equality; left the organization (1964) to form his own religious group and reaffirmed his conversion to orthodox Islam. He was shot dead by three Black Muslims in 1965.

◑ *see* Martin Luther King p. 277

MANDELA, NELSON (b. 1918)

South African Black Nationalist and Statesman Nelson Mandela joined the African National Congress in 1944, becoming one of its leaders in 1949. He was tried for treason but acquitted in 1961, but was jailed again in 1962 for five years. Whilst imprisoned he was tried for sabotage, treason and violent conspiracy and in 1964 was sentenced to life imprisonment, incarcerated at Robben Island Prison until February 1990. In March he was made deputy president of the ANC, replacing President Tambo in July. For his work to end apartheid he was awarded the Nobel Peace Prize in 1993 and the following year won South Africa's first all-race elections and established The Truth and Reconciliation Commission. He retired from politics in 1999. His book, *Long Walk to Freedom*, has become one of the most widely read autobiographies of modern times.

see Stephen Biko p. 272

MOTHER THERESA (1910–97)

'Mother Teresa of Calcutta' joined the Institute of the Blessed Virgin Mary in Ireland in 1928 and then travelled to India to work as a teacher. She studied nursing and founded the Order in 1948, adopting Indian citizenship. In 1963 she was recognized for her services to the people of India and was awarded, in 1971 the first Pope John XXIII Peace Prize and in 1979 the Nobel Peace Prize. The Order has continued serving the disadvantaged since her death in 1997, numbering 1,000 nuns operating 60 centres in Calcutta and 200 worldwide.

see Florence Nightingale p. 280

LEFT: Nelson Mandela, one of the leaders of the African National Congress (ANC).

NIGHTINGALE, FLORENCE (1820–1910)

English hospital reformer Florence Nightingale became known as the Lady with the Lamp. During the Crimean War she was based in the military hospitals of Turkey, managing to cope with severe overcrowding and the lack of basic necessities. In 1856 the Royal Commission on the Health of the Army was formed, leading to the foundation of the Army Medical School. She established, at St Thomas's Hospital, the Nightingale School for Nurses and in 1907 was the first woman to be awarded the Order of Merit.

◎ *see* Mother Theresa p. 279

▶ *RIGHT: Florence Nightingale.*

PANKHURST, EMMELINE (1858–1928)

At the start of the twentieth century women were not allowed to vote in political elections. In 1903 Emmeline Pankhurst founded the

Women's Social and Political Union to address the situation. Pankhurst launched the militant suffragette campaign in 1906, involving the organization of protests, which included hunger strikes by imprisoned campaigners, herself among them. Her daughters, Christabel and Sylvia, were keen supporters of her activities. Women finally received the right to vote in the year of her death.

◆ *see* Florence Nightingale p. 280

▶ *RIGHT: Emmeline Pankhurst is arrested.*

PERÓN, EVA (1919–52)

Eva was the wife of Argentine president Juan Perón. During her husband's first term, 'Evita' (as she was known) became a powerful political figure in her own right and a champion of the poor. She never held an official government post, but virtually ran the health and labour ministries. She awarded large wage increases to the unions and set up thousands of hospitals, schools and orphanages. Evita helped women get the vote and set up the Peronista Feminist Party in 1949. She was nominated for vice president in 1951, but was opposed by the army. She died of cancer soon after.

◆ *see* Eleanor Roosevelt p. 282

ROOSEVELT, ELEANOR (1884–1962)

Eleanor was the wife of Franklin D. Roosevelt, four times president of the USA. Eleanor greatly influenced the New Deal policies of his administration. She was chair of the UN commission on Human Rights 1946–51 and a major contributor to the Declaration of Human Rights.

▢ *see* Franklin D. Roosevelt p. 262

SCHINDLER, OSCAR (1908–1974)

Oscar Schindler was recruited by the German Intelligence Agency to collect information about the Polish. In Krakow he set up a factory, Deutsch Emailwaren Fabrik, but as the Nazi plan for the extermination of Jews escalated, he began protecting those working in his factory.

He smuggled food and medicines into the labour camp of Plaszow and did everything in his power to keep the Jews out of the concentration camps.

▢ *see* Adolf Hitler p. 248

◄ *LEFT: Liam Neeson as Oscar Schindler in Stephen Spielberg's Oscar-winning film, Schindler's List.*

SCHWEITZER, ALBERT (1875–1965)

Schweitzer vowed in 1896 that he would change his life at 30 years of age in order to serve humanity. He qualified as a doctor and in 1913 set out to fight leprosy at Lambarene in Africa, where he remained. He was awarded the Nobel Peace Prize in 1952. His work *Quest of the*

Historical Jesus was widely read as it continued the belief current in Protestant theology of his time that it was very difficult, if indeed possible, to discover the historical figure Jesus; Jesus was masked by the 'Christ of faith'. Like other theologians he moulded his views of Jesus to his own convictions.

◆ see Mother Theresa p. 279

▲ ABOVE: The German theologian and philanthropist Albert Schweitzer was awarded both the Nobel Peace Prize and the Order of Merit for his humanitarian efforts in developing countries.

TUTU, DESMOND (b. 1931)

Archbishop of Cape Town 1981–96, and general secretary of the South African Council of Churches 1979–84. He was awarded the Nobel Peace Prize (1984) for his struggle against apartheid.

◆ see Nelson Mandela p. 279

SCIENCE, TECHNOLOGY & INDUSTRY

BAIRD, JOHN LOGIE (1888–1946)

The television started life as the brainchild of Scottish inventor John Logie Baird. The first working prototype was demonstrated in 1926. It was primitive, but showed that the idea worked. Eventually the familiar television, using a cathode-ray tube, became the preferred format. The design has gone on to be used for computer monitors. By 1928 Baird had also perfected the workings of colour television.

◆ *see* Thomas Edison p. 289

BARNARD, CHRISTIAAN (b. 1922)

On 3 December 1967, the South African surgeon and pioneer of cardiac medicine Christiaan Barnard performed the first human heart transplant. The patient was a 54-year-old man and the procedure was a tricky one. Although such surgery had been attempted before, it had never proved successful. The operation took place at the Groote Schuur Hospital, South Africa, and the patient lived for a groundbreaking 18 days.

◆ *see* Alexander Fleming p. 290

BELL, ALEXANDER GRAHAM (1847–1922)

Scottish inventor Alexander Graham Bell demonstrated the telephone for the first time in 1876 in the United States. The inventor was Scottish-born, but moved across the Atlantic to Canada in 1870, with his family. He invented the telephone by assembling and perfecting various devices invented by others and was able to transmit the first-ever spoken message via an electrical wire.

◆ *see* Guglielmo Marconi p. 298

▶ RIGHT: Polish-born scientist Marie Curie studied the nature of uranium rays and discovered the elements polonium and radium.

BOHR, NIELS (1885–1962)

The Danish physicist Niels Bohr is regarded as the father of quantum mechanics and was one of the most influential scientists of the twentieth century. In 1911 Bohr went to work with J. J. Thomson in Cambridge and later with Ernest Rutherford in Manchester, where he developed a model of the atom based on electron orbits that obeyed the rules of the then-new quantum theory. He was awarded the Nobel Prize for this work in 1922. Bohr famously entered a long-running debate with Albert Einstein over the meaning of the new theory, developing what became known as the Copenhagen Theory. During World War II, after working tirelessly to help Danish Jews escape the German occupation, Bohr himself escaped to the US, where he worked on the atomic bomb project. He later returned to Denmark, devoting his life to promoting peaceful uses for atomic energy.

◆ *see* Ernest Rutherford p. 300

CURIE, MARIE (1867–1934) AND PIERRE (1859–1906)

Polish scientists Marie and Pierre Curie were pioneers in the study of radiation. In fact, they shared the Nobel Prize for Physics with Henri Becquerel, in 1903, for the discovery of radiation. They discovered the radioactive elements polonium and radium in pieces of pitchblende, managing to isolate samples in 1902. Marie went on to win the Nobel Prize for Chemistry in 1911 for her continued work in the field.

◆ *see* Alexander Fleming p. 290

EDDINGTON, SIR ARTHUR (1882–1944)

Arthur Edington was born into a Quaker family in Kendal, Cumbria. He had a brilliant passage through school, college and university, becoming Plumian professor at Cambridge in 1913, where he spent the remainder of his career. He was one of the earliest and authoritative proponents of Albert Einstein's theory of relativity and was closely involved in one of the expeditions to photograph the solar eclipse of 1919, which demonstrated the bending of light by a gravitational field, in this case, the Sun's. Eddington worked in many areas of astronomy, such as stellar dynamics and the nature of the interstellar medium, but one in which he played a major role was the application of physical and mathematical principles to describe the structure a star. Towards the end of his life he devoted his considerable intellectual powers to a search for connections between the fundamental constants of nature.

◻ see Albert Einstein p. 290

EDISON, THOMAS ALVA (1847–1931)

American inventor Thomas Alva Edison first made his fortune by selling a machine he had invented in 1869 that used a paper 'ticker' tape for sending electrical information on stocks and shares. With the proceeds, Edison established his industrial research laboratory that served him for the rest of his life. In the laboratory he had a team of dedicated technicians who would try things out time and time again until an idea was perfected into a working prototype. His most celebrated invention was the electric light bulb, but among his other inventions was the phonograph record player.

◻ see John Logie Baird p. 286

◀ LEFT: Thomas Edison invented the first commercially viable electric bulb.

▶ RIGHT: Albert Einstein formulated theories about the nature and structure of the universe which permanently changed our view of cosmology.

EINSTEIN, ALBERT (1879–1955)

Swiss-born mathematician Albert Einstein's work in mathematical physics astounded the world. Prior to Einstein's theories, human understanding of gravity and other physical phenomena had been based on Newtonian laws.

Einstein published his own theories, based on mathematical formulae, that demonstrated relationships between time, light, mass, gravity and space. Unlike Newton's laws, however, they could not be easily proven by experimentation, even though they worked on paper. Other scientists, such as Arthur Eddington, eventually began to show that Einstein was correct in his assertions.

Einstein's best-known theory is his theory of general relativity, published in 1905. It shows that motion and mass have relative, rather than absolute, characters, because of interdependence between matter, time and space. His famous formula $E = mc^2$ demonstrates that mass and energy are equivalent.

◆ see Sir Arthur Eddington p. 289

FLEMING, ALEXANDER (1881–1955)

In 1941, during World War II, commercial production of penicillin began. The theatre of war was the perfect setting to show how remarkable this antibiotic was at combating bacterially infected wounds. Alexander Fleming was the man behind the discovery of penicillin. He had been researching pathogenic *Staphylococci* bacteria and noticed that a mould called *Penicillium notatum* secreted a substance that inhibited growth in the bacteria. He always claimed that the discovery was more luck than

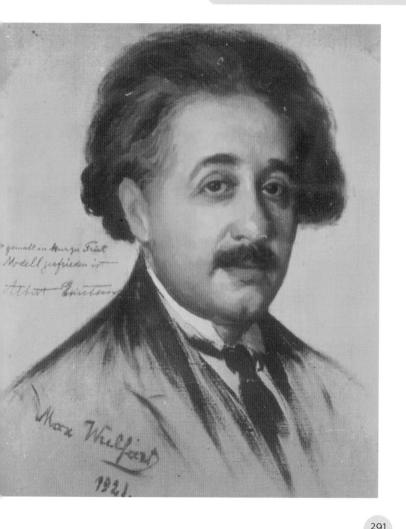

gemalt in kurzer Frist
Modell zufrieden ist —
Albert Einstein

Max Wulfaes
1921.

judgement – he had simply left the bacteria in its dishes when he went away on holiday and on his return noticed the mould that had grown around it. He won the Nobel Prize for Medicine in 1945.

◆ see Marie Curie p. 287

▶ RIGHT: Sir Alexander Fleming, the British medical scientist and bacteriologist.

▶ RIGHT: The US automobile manufacturer Henry Ford sitting in his first prototype model of a car.

FORD, HENRY (1863–1947)

In 1903 American industrialist and automobile pioneer Henry Ford founded the Ford Motor Company and in 1908–09 developed the famous Model T vehicle (discontinued after sales of 15 million in 1927). In 1913 he began using standardized interchangeable parts and assembly-line methods of manufacture, which became widespread practices throughout American industry, greatly increasing productivity. A pacifist, Ford visited Europe in 1915–16 to try to end the war. During World War II the Ford Company manufactured 8,000 bombers.

■ *see* Bill Gates p. 294

► *RIGHT: A sixth-grader shows Bill Gates the computer she uses at a school in Harlem, New York City.*

GATES, BILL (b. 1955)

American businessman Bill Gates was the co-founder in 1975, chairman and chief executive of the Microsoft Corporation, which introduced such innovations as MS-DOS, the operating system for the IBM personal computer, and Microsoft Word software. Gates' technical brilliance and business acumen have made him unimaginably wealthy (£37.5 billion in 2001). The US government, however, laid monopoly charges against Microsoft.

◆ *see* Henry Ford p. 293

HAWKING, STEPHEN (b. 1942)

The English theoretical physicist Stephen Hawking was born in Oxford. Having graduated from the university there he moved to Cambridge to study for his PhD. He was made Lucasian Professor of Mathematics there in 1980. Hawking's work has been an attempt to synthesize the theories of gravity and quantum mechanics. After early work on relativity, Hawking concentrated on the problem of gravitational singularities, publishing important work on black holes and the Big Bang.

In 1988 Hawking published *A Brief History of Time*, a popular account of the current thinking in cosmology. The book was an outstanding success, reprinted ten times in the first year of publication and several times since then. It was another major achievement for a man afflicted by a crippling motor neurone disease, which has confined him to a wheelchair and requires him to talk by means of a voice synthesizer. (*See over for illustration.*)

◆ *see* Niels Bohr p. 287

▲ *ABOVE: Author and scientist Stephen Hawking.*

HEISENBERG, WERNER (1901–76)

In 1927 the German physicist Werner Heisenberg drew up the 'Uncertainty Principle' of quantum mechanics, which states that an atomic particle cannot have a measurable position and momentum simultaneously, because at nanoscale the very act of measuring will disturb the particle so as to nullify the measurement. The theory was a significant turning-point in the developement of quantum physics.

◆ *see* Stephen Hawking p. 294

▶ RIGHT: *Werner Heisenberg's Uncertainty Principle has become fundamental to understanding quantum physics.*

HUBBLE, EDWIN (1889–1953)

The American astronomer Edwin Powell Hubble studied law at the University of Chicago and was a Rhodes Scholar at the University of Oxford from 1910 to 1913. Back in the United States he decided against a career in law and took up astronomy. After military service during World War II he took a post at the Mount Wilson Observatory, where he remained until his death in 1953. Using Cepheid Variable stars Hubble determined the distance to the Andromeda galaxy in 1924. From his study of galaxies he proposed an evolutionary sequence beginning with near-circular elliptical galaxies and moving through increasing ellipticity to reach a basic form of spiral galaxy. the sequence. Hubble's basic forms are still used to define galactic types. In 1929 Hubble proposed what is now known as Hubble's Law, implying that we live in an expanding universe.

◆ see Albert Einstein p. 290

LISTER, JOSEPH (1827–1912)

The English surgeon Joseph Lister was the first person to introduce sterilization procedures into his operating room. He sprayed phenol (carbolic acid) on to wounds and heated instruments before use so that the environment was as antiseptic as possible. He was influenced by the work of Louis Pasteur.

◆ see Alexander Fleming p. 290

MARCONI, GUGLIELMO (1874–1937)

In the late 1890s the Italian Guglielmo Marconi developed radio communications, or the 'wireless' as it became known. He perfected the system by 1897 and was able to raise the funds to establish a communications company which was transmitting between England

and France by 1899. Transatlantic transmissions were possible by 1901 and the wireless would soon become a vital piece of kit in shipping and warfare communications.

◆ see Thomas Edison p. 289

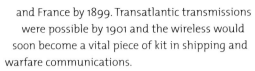

◀ LEFT: Guglielmo Marconi produced the precursor of the radio, a type of wireless telegraph. He had been much influenced by Hertz's theories of electromagnetic waves.

PLANCK, MAX (1858–1947)

The German physicist Max Planck grew up in Munich, but studied in Berlin under some of the most influential physicists of the nineteenth century. He received his doctorate at the age of 21 and soon afterwards joined the faculty at the University of Munich, where he remained until his retirement in 1926.

Planck's radical quantum theory took several years to be accepted. As an elder stateman of science, Planck resisted the Nazis during the 1930s. He lost his two sons during World War II: one was killed in action, the other was executed after being accused of plotting to assassinate Hitler. Planck was rescued by the Allies in 1945 and spent the last two years of his life honoured around the world.

◆ see Albert Einstein p. 290

RÖNTGEN, WILHELM (1845–1923)

In 1895, while experimenting with the passage of electricity through gases, German scientist Wilhelm Röntgen noticed that his experiment was causing a coated photographic screen to fluoresce. He then discovered that the mysterious rays would pass through some substances but not others. He called them X-rays and began to experiment with photographic plates. X-ray scanning revolutionized medicine by allowing physicians to see inside the body without physical investigation. Röntgen was awarded the Nobel Prize for Physics in 1901.

see Marie Curie p. 287

RUTHERFORD, ERNEST (1871–1937)

Born in New Zealand, Ernest Rutherford was to become one of the most influential figures of twentieth-century science. By the time he had demonstrated the existence of the atomic nucleus, though his study of alpha-particle scattering, he had already won a Nobel Prize for chemistry. he was later to go on to make many significant contributions to physics.

Rutherford was knighted in 1914 and took over from J. J. Thomson as Director of the Cavendish Laboratory in Cambridge in 1919. He was president of the Royal Society from 1925 to 1930, and was created baron Rutherford of Nelson (after his birthplace) in 1931, enabling him to take up a place in the House of Lords.

His greatest mistake was the belief that nuclear power could never be realized. He famously descibed as 'moonshine' the notion that humanity could ever harness the energy trapped within atomic nuclei. He died two years before the discovery of nuclear fission.

see Niels Bohr p. 287

SALK, JONAS (1914–95)

In 1954, after many years of research, the New York-born virologist, Dr Jonas Salk developed a vaccine against poliomyelitis. The disease, its name commonly shortened to polio, would at best leave its victms severely crippled and at worst kill them. In the 1950s, cases of polio reached epidemic proportions, with 59,000 cases reported in 1952 alone. News of the Salk vaccine was made public on 12 April 1955 and Dr Salk

▲ ABOVE: Dr Jonas Salk holding bottles containing the culture used to create the polio vaccine.

was hailed as a miracle worker – inoculations began the very same day. Less than a month later, however, the inoculation programme was stopped, after it was discovered that 204 people who had been given the vaccine had afterwards developed the disease; 11 of them had died. Subsequently, the Salk vaccine underwent extremely intensive testing before inoculations resumed in 1957. From this time, the incidence of poliomyelitis began to fall until, in industrialized countries, it was virtually eradicated.

◆ see Alexander Fleming p. 290

EXPLORATION & DISCOVERY

ALDRIN, EDWIN 'BUZZ' (b. 1930)

American astronaut Buzz Aldrin fought in the Korean War before entering the astronaut training programme. In 1966, as co-pilot of Gemini 12, Aldrin achieved a record five-hour space walk. In 1969, during the Apollo 11 lunar mission, he became the second man to set foot on the Moon.

◆ *see* Neil Armstrong p. 305

AMUNDSEN, ROALD (1872–1928)

In 1903–05 Norwegian polar explorer Roald Amundsen achieved the first voyage through the North-West Passage in a single vessel, the sloop *Gjøa*, having spent two winters on King William Island calculating the exact position of the North Magnetic Pole. In 1910 he set sail for Antarctica. On 14 December 1911 he and four companions, using dog-sledges, became the first men to reach the South Pole, a month ahead of Captain Robert Scott.

◆ *see* Robert Scott p. 309

ARMSTRONG, NEIL (b. 1930)

A former fighter pilot in the Korean War in 1962, American astronaut Neil Armstrong became the first civilian to enter the astronaut training programme. In 1966 he was command pilot of the Gemini 8 mission, which achieved the first physical joining of two orbiting spacecraft. In July 1969 Armstrong, as commander of the Apollo 11 lunar mission, became the first person to set foot on the Moon. His companions were Edwin 'Buzz' Aldrin and Michael Collins.

◆ *see* Edwin 'Buzz' Aldrin p. 305

◀ *LEFT: American astronaut Edwin 'Buzz' Aldrin, one of a select group of men to have walked on the Moon.*

CARNARVON, LORD (1866–1923)

George Edward Stanhope Molyneux Herbert, 5th Earl of Carnarvon, a keen amateur Egyptologist, was the sponsor whose money made possible Howard Carter's historic excavations in the Valley of Kings. If his popular fame has outlasted that of the archeologist himself, that is because his death so soon after Carter's discovery of Tutankhamen's tomb in 1922 led to fevered speculation that he had fallen victim to the pharaoh's curse.

⬛ *see* Sir Edmund Hillary p. 307

EARHART, AMELIA (1897–1937)

On 17 June 1928, Amelia Earhart became the first woman to fly across the Atlantic Ocean, although she did so only as a passenger. In 1932, she took the controls herself and became the first woman to pilot an aircraft, a Lockheed 'Vega', on a transatlantic flight. From then on, Amelia Earhart belonged to an elite of aviation pioneers who initiated what later became the world's commercial air routes. Earhart was the first pilot – male or female – to fly alone from Hawaii to California, in 1935. Two years later, with navigator Frederick Noonan, Earhart made an attempt at flying around the world, but their Lockheed Electra 10E aircraft apparently ran out of fuel and crashed in the Pacific somewhere between New Guinea and Howland Island. Neither Earhart nor Noonan was ever seen again.

⬛ *see* Charles Lindbergh p. 307

GAGARIN, YURI (1934–68)

Russian cosmonaut Yuri Gagarin was the first person to travel in space. In 1961 Gagarin rode aboard the satellite *Vostok I* on a single orbit of the Earth at 27,400 kph (17,000 mph) between 180 and 327 km (112 and 203 miles) above the Earth's surface. Gagarin was killed in the crash of a test aircraft.

⬛ *see* Neil Armstrong p. 305

HILLARY, SIR EDMUND (b. 1919)

A strong climber, in 1953 New Zealand mountaineer and Antarctic explorer Edmund Hillary joined the British Mount Everest Expedition, led by John Hunt. On 29 May he and Sherpa Tenzing Norgay became the first known climbers to reach the summit, for which he was later knighted. In 1955, as leader of the New Zealand part of the British Commonwealth Trans-Antarctic Expedition led by Vivian Fuchs, he crossed the continent by snow tractor, the first to cross overland since Robert Scott in 1912. Hillary's Himalayan Trust has built schools, hospitals and airstrips for the Sherpa people and planted new forests.

■ see Robert Scott p. 309

LINDBERGH, CHARLES (1902–74)

American aviator Charles Lindbergh was the first person to make a non-stop solo flight across the Atlantic. Lindbergh took off in his single-engine monoplane *Spirit of St Louis* from Long Island on 20 May 1927 and landed at Le Bourget Airport near Paris 33 hours and 32 minutes later, thereby claiming a $25,000 prize. In 1933 Lindbergh surveyed over 48,000 km (30,000 miles) for transatlantic air routes and landing fields. Being a public hero proved to have tragic consequences, however, when his baby son was kidnapped and murdered, prompting the Lindbergh's move to the UK. (*See over for illustration.*)

■ see Amelia Earhart p. 306

NANSEN, FRIDTJOF (1861–1930)

Norwegian explorer and statesman Fridtjof Nansen made the first crossing of Greenland. Study of Arctic currents convinced him that a ship frozen into the ice would drift over the North Pole. He attempted this in the ship *Fram* but slowness of drift forced Nansen and a

companion to strike out for the Pole by dog-sled. They reached 86°14′, a new record. Nansen became a Nobel laureate for his work following the Russian Revolution.

◆ *see* Roald Amundsen p. 305

PEARY, ROBERT (1856–1920)

American polar explorer Robert Peary made seven polar expeditions, developing the Peary System of Arctic travel, which included Inuit (Eskimo) survival skills and the establishment of supply depots. He crossed northern Greenland and contributed greatly to knowledge of that region, of glaciation and of Inuit ethnology. After three unsuccessful attempts Peary, with his assistant Matthew Henson and four Inuit, reached the North Pole (or near it) on 6 April 1909, having made a final dash with dog-sledges in a spell of fine weather. Dr Frederick Cook claimed to have reached the Pole a year earlier but Peary's records were accepted as genuine.

◆ *see* Robert Scott p. 309

SCOTT, ROBERT (1868–1912)

British naval officer and Antarctic explorer Robert Falcon Scott commanded the British National Antarctic Expedition of 1901–04 and in 1910 mounted a private expedition to Antarctica aboard the *Terra Nova*. After making preparations and scientific observations for a year, in November 1911 Scott's party of five set out for the Pole. Ponies and motorized vehicles proved useless, so the team hauled their own sledges to reach the Pole on 16 January 1912, only to find that the Norwegian

◀ LEFT: Pioneering aviator Charles Lindbergh, who made the first solo flight across the Atlantic.

Roald Amundsen had got there a month earlier. The return journey was dogged by appalling weather and resulted in the deaths of the entire party. Scott's diaries preserve the last few days of their expedition, knowing that they were going to die. The last entry reads: 'For God's sake look after our people.'

◆ *see* Roald Amundsen p. 305

◄ *LEFT: Robert Falcon Scott.*

SHACKLETON, ERNEST (1874–1922)

Irish-born Ernest Shackleton was a junior officer with the National Antarctic Expedition of 1901–04, led by Robert Scott. On this expedition, Scott and Shackleton made an epic journey to arrive within 772 km (480 miles) of the South Pole. Four years later, leading his own Antarctic expedition, Shackleton set a further record for the closest approach to the South Pole: 156.2 km (97 miles). Another of Shackleton's expeditions, which took place in 1914–16, nearly ended in disaster after his ship the Endurance was crushed in the ice. Shackleton and his men used boats and sledges to cover the 161 km (100 miles) to Elephant Island, off the westernmost tip of Antarctica. Afterwards, with five others, Shackleton made a harrowing journey of 1,287 km (800 miles) to reach South Georgia, a dependency of the Falkland Islands. Shackleton, who had been knighted in 1909, was again in South Georgia, planning a fourth expedition, when he died of a heart attack on 5 January 1922.

◆ see Robert Peary p. 309

WRIGHT BROTHERS

American brothers Wilbur (1867–1912) and Orville (1871–1948), were the pioneers of powered flight. While running a bicycle repair business they experimented with gliders and the effects of air pressure on wing surfaces. From their own calculations the built propellers, a wind tunnel and finally a machine with a 12-horsepower motor, which they called the Flyer. On 17 December 1903 they made the first controlled powered-aeroplane flights. They made hundreds of flights in the succeeding years, the longest lasting some 38 minutes.

◆ see Charles Lindbergh p. 307

GLOSSARY

ACADEMY AWARDS

The most prominent US film awards, better known as Oscars; the awards are granted annually by the Academy of Motion Picture Arts and Sciences and contain categories for Best Actor/Actress, Best Director and Best Screenplay.

ANSCHLUSS

The name given to the invasion and annexation of Austria by Nazi Germany in March 1938 in the lead-up to World War II.

APARTHEID

An Afrikaans word used to describe segregation in South Africa, based on a belief in white superiority.

ART NOUVEAU

A school of art and architecture originating in France at the end of the nineteenth century, characterized by naturalistic forms and sinuous outlines.

ARTS AND CRAFTS

An all-encompassing artistic movement begun towards the end of the nineteenth century and led by William Morris in Britain. The movement touched all forms of art, including architecture and gardening.

BAUHAUS

A German style of architecture pioneered by Walter Gropius around 1918.

BAY OF PIGS INVASION

A US planned and funded invasion by armed Cuban exiles in an attempt to overthrow the socialist government run by Fidel Castro. The invasion failed.

BLITZ

The name given to the German air attack on London and other British cities at the beginning of World War II, in which many buildings were destroyed and civilian lives lost.

BOER WAR

The war between the South African Boers (Dutch settlers) and British colonists between 1899 and 1902.

BUDDHISM

An Eastern religion based on the teachings of the sixth-century Buddha, founded in the destruction of mortal desires and the encouragement of following virtuous paths to Enlightenment.

COLD WAR

The name given to the period after World War II marked by military tension between western alliances and the Soviet Union.

COMMONWEALTH GAMES

A multi-sport event held every four years, involving athletes from the British Commonwealth and first held in 1930.

COMMUNISM

A classless system of economics in which the production of food and goods is a communal activity for the general good. The principles of Communism were popularized by Karl Marx.

CONSERVATIVE PARTY

The largest centre-right political party in the United Kingdom, in government under the leadership of Margaret Thatcher until its dramatic overthrow in the 1997 General Election.

CONSTRUCTIVISM

A Russian artistic movement founded by Vladimir Tatlin, which favours 'pure' art with no social functions.

CRIMEAN WAR

Campaign fought in 1854–56 between Russia and an alliance of France, Britain and the Ottoman Empire in a dispute about the guardianship of several Palestinian regions. Florence Nightingale made her name nursing the wounded soldiers during this war.

CUBAN MISSILE CRISIS

A Cold-War conflict between the Soviet Union and the United States over the Soviet ownership of nuclear missiles. It lasted for 13 days during which the world came close to nuclear war.

CUBISM

An avant-garde artistic movement begun by Braque and essence of which is that instead of viewing a subject from a fixed angle, it is broken up into several facets which can be viewed simultaneously.

CULTURAL REVOLUTION

A campaign launched by China's Chairman Mao in 1966 in an attempt to dispose of his political rivals.

DADAISM

A post-World War I artistic and cultural movement originating in Switzerland.

D-DAY LANDINGS

The unofficial name given to the Allied offensive Operation Overlord, in which thousands of Allied troops were landed on the beaches of Normandy in a final push to relieve France from German occupation.

DE STIJL

An artistic movement that favoured pure abstraction and simplicity, reducing subjects to plain geometric shapes along with primary colours, along with black and white. Its leading exponent was Piet Mondrian.

DEMOCRATIC PARTY

The older of the two main political parties in the US. The other is the Republican Party.

DER BLAUE REITER

'The Blue Rider'. A group of German artists established by Wassily Kandinsky in 1911, whose interest focused on medieval art and primitivism.

EUROPEAN ECONOMIC COMMUNITY

An international organization founded in 1957 and ratified by the Treaty of Rome, which deals with European policy voted on by elected members of its affiliated countries. The 'Economic' has now been dropped.

EXISTENTIALISM

A philosophical movement expounded by the works of Jean-Paul Sartre, which emphasizes individuality, freedom and subjectivity.

FASCISM

An authoritarian political movement reaching its height in the 1930s and 1940s under leaders such as Joseph Stalin, in which democracy was abandoned in favour of nationalistic ideology.

FAUVISM

A short-lived artistic movement that was a precursor to Modernism, characterized by the use of deep colour and a dominance of the paint itself.

FESTIVAL OF BRITAIN

A celebration in the 1950s of British and Commonwealth optimism, marked by the building of the arts centre on London's South Bank.

FIVE-YEAR PLANS

A programme of reforms established in the Soviet Union by Joseph Stalin, intended to bring about swift improvement in the country's economy through a process of centralization.

FUTURISM

An art movement of the early twentieth century, largely followed in Italy and Russia, which explored a variety of mediums and methods of expression.

GRAMMY AWARDS

An annual award presented by the American Recording Academy for outstanding achievements in music.

GRAND SLAM

In tennis, winning the Grand Slam means simultaneously holding the titles for the Australian Open, French Open, US Open and British Open (Wimbledon).

GREAT LEAP FORWARD

One of Chairman Mao's programmes of reform based on the supply of cheap labour to increase China's industrialization.

IMPRESSIONISM

An artistic movement of the mid to late nineteenth century, established in France, in which the subjects are painted in vague dashes of light and colour intended to give an impression rather than accurately depict the detail. The name is taken from one of Claude Monet's paintings, *Impression: Sunrise*.

KHMER ROUGE

The name given to the communist organization in Cambodia ruled by Pol Pot, and which was characterized by widespread genocide.

LABOUR PARTY

Centre-left political party in Britain, currently in government and led by prime minister Tony Blair.

LIVE AID

A music concert that took place in 1985 involving musicians from the UK and US in an unprecedented abandonment of egos. It was organized by Bob Geldof to raise money to help famine victims in Ethiopia.

LUFTWAFFE

The German air force during World War II. The Luftwaffe took on the British RAF in the Battle of Britain, and was also responsible for the Blitz on London in 1940.

MARXISM

A school of thought established by Karl Marx in the late nineteenth century and based on the principles of socialism.

NAZISM

The German fascist regime under Adolf Hitler in the 1930s and 1940s, taken from the National Socialist Party, of which Hitler was head. The Nazis sought to build an empire for the Aryan race, resulting in persecution of groups such as Jews.

NOBEL PRIZE

A series of Prizes established by Alfred Nobel, awarded for outstanding contributions in global fields, such as Medicine, Literature, Physics and Peace.

OP ART

A style of abstract art popular in the 1960s based on dramatic visual effects that can be confusing to the viewer's eye.

PALESTINIAN LIBERATION ORGANIZATION

A political movement of Palestinian Arabs, established by Yasser Arafat in 1958 to try and establish an independent Palestinian state.

POET LAUREATE

In Britain, the poet appointed to the royal household, who is expected to provide poems for national occasions.

POP ART

An American artistic style prevalent in the 1950s and led by Andy Warhol, which imitated the style and techniques of commercial art and the mass media.

PRE-RAPHAELITES

An artistic movement begun in the mid nineteenth century, which shunned the decadent conventions used since the time of the artist Raphael and returned to moral subjects painted in a realistic manner. The Pre-Raphaelite style continued to influence artists into the twentieth century.

RASTAFARI

A Jamaican religious youth movement based on the divinity of Ras Tafari. Males grow their hair into dreadlocks and wear woollen caps.

REPUBLICAN PARTY

One of the two major political parties in the US. The current president George W. Bush is a Republican.

ROCK AND ROLL HALL OF FAME

An American museum celebrating the stars of rock and pop music. Induction into the Hall of Fame is considered a great honour amongst musicians.

RUSSIAN REVOLUTION

The name given to the events in 1917 that resulted in the overthrow of the Russian monarchy under Tsar Nicholas II by the Bolsheviks.

SERIE A

Italy's premiership soccer league, amongst the best-regarded in the sport.

SPANISH CIVIL WAR

War waged 1936–39 in Spain between the rebels (Nacionales) and the Republican government. The rebels won and the dictator Francisco Franco took control of the country.

ST VALENTINE'S DAY MASSACRE

The 14 February assassination of seven men in the gang warfare waged under Al Capone during the period of Prohibition in the US.

STALINISM

The political and economic system initiated by Soviet leader Joseph Stalin, and which included the Five-Year Plans.

STREAM-OF-CONSCIOUSNESS

A literary technique that became popular under writers such as James Joyce and Virginia Woolf in the 1920s, in which the writing takes the form of the narrator's thought processes.

SUFFRAGISM

The belief in the extension of equal rights to women and the working classes, who were traditionally denied the right to vote at the beginning of the twentieth century.

SURREALISM

A twentieth-century art movement, which deployed fantastical distorted images and incongruous juxtapositions to represent unconscious thoughts and dreams. Its leading exponent was Salvador Dali.

SYMBOLISM

An artistic movement driven by the belief that art should incorporate absolute truths that can only be accessed by indirect methods, and thus endowed objects and words with symbolic meanings.

TONY AWARDS

The colloquial name for the Antoinette Perry Awards, an annual American award ceremony celebrating achievements in theatre.

TURNER PRIZE

Britain's most publicized annual prize awarded to a British artist, named after the painter J. M. W. Turner and organized by the Tate Gallery in London. It was founded in 1984.

US OPEN

The name given to both tennis and golf championships held in America and part of the Grand Slam tournaments in each sport.

VIETNAM WAR

The war fought between 1964 and 1975 in South Vietnam, between a South Vietnam and US coalition against Communist China and North Vietnam (the Viet Cong). The continued US participation in the war was widely condemned, even by US citizens.

WATERGATE

An American political scandal that took place in 1972 during Richard Nixon's tenure as president, in which five men were caught breaking into the Watergate Offices in Washington, DC to bug the building and allegedly to photograph documents. The president himself was implicated in the scandal.

WIMBLEDON

The tennis championships (the British Open) held annually in South London and drawing international players.

WORLD CUP

A four-yearly soccer tournament between national teams to determine a world champion. The World Cup is the pinnacle of international soccer.

WORLD WAR I

The name given to the global conflict that raged between 1914 and 1918, instigated by the assassination of the Austrian Archduke Franz Ferdinand in Serbia and Germany's subsequent alliance with Austro-Hungary against the union of Britain, France and Belgium.

WORLD WAR II

The war between 1939 and 1945 instigated by the rise of Nazism in Germany under Adolf Hitler and his invasion of Poland, which caused Britain and France to enter the war, and later the US to join after the Japanese attack on Pearl Harbor.

YALTA CONFERENCE

The meeting held on 4–11 February 1945 between the heads of government of the US, the UK and the USSR – Roosevelt, Churchill and Stalin – in which post-war reparations were discussed.

BIBLIOGRAPHY

Albee, Edward (foreword), *Icons and Idols: A Photographer's Chronicle of the Arts 1960–1995*, Amphoto Books, 1998

Burham, Rosemary, et al, *Journeys of the Great Explorers*, AA Publishing, 1992

Cady, Barbara, *Icons of the 20th Century*, Hardie Grant Publishing, 1998

Cochrane, Jennifer, *An Illustrated History of Medicine*, Tiger Books, 1996

Dyson, James, *History of Great Inventions*, Robinson Publishing, 2002

Fussell, Paul, *The Great War and Modern Memory*, Oxford University Press, 2000

Gilbert, Martin, *Second World War*, HarperCollins Publishers, 2000

Hiller, Bevis, *The Style of the Century*, Herbert Press, 1998

Johnson, Holly, *Pop and Rock: Rock and Pop*, Absolute Press, 2003

Katz, Ephraim, et al, *The Macmillan International Film Encyclopedia*, Macmillan, 2001

Lawson, Susannah, *The 20th Century Art Book*, Phaidon Press, 1999

Lewis, Brenda Ralph, *Modern History: A Source Book*, Flame Tree Publishing, 2003

Maltby, Richard and Ian Craven, *Hollywood Cinema*, Blackwell Publishers, 2003

Noyer, Paul du, *The Illustrated Encyclopedia of Music*, Flame Tree Publishing, 2003

Paten, Ian, *Who's Who in British Sport: The Comprehensive Directory of Today's Sports Personalities*, Virgin Books, 1994

Paxman, Jeremy (foreword), *20th Century Day by Day*, Dorling Kindersley, 2000

Pilger, John, *The New Rulers of the World*, Verso Books, 2003

Reid, S. et al, *The Usborne Book of Famous Lives*, Usborne Publishing, 2002

Roberts, J. M., *The Penguin History of the Twentieth Century*, Penguin, 2000

Robertson, A.H. and J. G. Merrills, *Human Rights in the World*, Manchester University Press, 1996

Sadie, Stanley (ed.), *The Classical Music Encyclopedia*, HarperCollins Publishers, 2000

ACKNOWLEDGEMENTS

Anthony Oliver: 40

The Art Archive: Co of Merchants, City of Edinburgh: 243; RAMC Historical Museum/HarperCollins Publishers: 280

British Film Institute: 116–117

Christie's Images: Private Collection: 7, 51; Private Collection/Bridgeman Art Gallery: 10–11, 16

Foundry Arts: 78–79, 81, 96, 111, 113, 121, 124

Getty Images/Allsport: 4–5, 136, 137, 140, 142, 143, 144, 146, 151, 153, 154, 156, 158, 161, 163, 164, 167, 170, 172, 174, 177, 187, 188, 190, 192, 195, 197, 198, 199, 201, 202, 204, 205, 206, 209, 214, 215, 222, 226–227; David Cannon: 224–225; Tony Duffy: 194, 220; Hulton Getty: 138–139; Adrian Murrell: 148; Gary M. Prior: 176; Ben Radford: 182–183

Impact Photos: Mohamed Ansar: 230, 273; John Arthur: 266, 278; Julian Calder: 67; Piers Cavendish: 231, 234; John Cole: 94; Mark Henley: 270–271, 275; Tom Webster: 259

Mary Evans Picture Library: 70, 86, 92, 99, 101, 103, 228–229, 233, 245, 248, 251, 254, 257, 260, 261, 267, 276, 284–285, 288, 292, 293, 297, 299, 302–303, 308; Explorer Archives: 291; National Portrait Gallery: 25, 68; Sigmund Freud Copyrights: 274

Popperfoto: 169

Topham Picturepoint: 6, 8, 9, 13, 19, 20, 22, 24, 27, 29, 31, 33, 35, 36, 38, 42, 44, 47, 48, 53, 57, 58, 63, 65, 75, 80, 91, 109, 127, 129, 132–133, 134, 149, 160, 178, 180, 185, 211, 218–219, 232, 237, 239, 240, 241, 246, 247, 250, 252, 264, 265, 269, 281, 282, 283, 287, 295, 296, 301, 304, 310; Robert Millard/PAL: 55

Sonya Newland is a writer and editor, and has contributed to numerous volumes on historical subjects, ranging from ancient Egypt to the British royal family and from reference encyclopedias to children's books. She has a particular interest in modern history, and has most recently worked on titles covering the two World Wars, scientific discoveries of the twentieth century and popular music since the 1950s.

INDEX